The Wings of Isis

A temple by temple guide to
The Magic and Ritual of Egypt

First published by O Books, 2009
O Books is an imprint of John Hunt Publishing Ltd., The Bothy, Deershot Lodge, Park Lane, Ropley,
Hants, SO24 0BE, UK
office1@o-books.net
www.o-books.net

Distribution in:	South Africa
	Alternative Books
UK and Europe	altbook@peterhyde.co.za
Orca Book Services	Tel: 021 555 4027 Fax: 021 447 1430
orders@orcabookservices.co.uk	
Tel: 01202 665432 Fax: 01202 666219	Text copyright Lady Brenda McKoy 2008
Int. code (44)	
	Design: Stuart Davies
USA and Canada	
NBN	ISBN: 978 1 84694 218 1
custserv@nbnbooks.com	
Tel: 1 800 462 6420 Fax: 1 800 338 4550	All rights reserved. Except for brief quotations
	in critical articles or reviews, no part of this
Australia and New Zealand	book may be reproduced in any manner without
Brumby Books	prior written permission from the publishers.
sales@brumbybooks.com.au	
Tel: 61 3 9761 5535 Fax: 61 3 9761 7095	The rights of Lady Brenda McKoy as author have
	been asserted in accordance with the
Far East (offices in Singapore, Thailand,	Copyright, Designs and Patents Act 1988.
Hong Kong, Taiwan)	
Pansing Distribution Pte Ltd	
kemal@pansing.com	A CIP catalogue record for this book is available
Tel: 65 6319 9939 Fax: 65 6462 5761	from the British Library.

Printed by Digital Book Print

O Books operates a distinctive and ethical publishing philosophy in
all areas of its business, from its global network of authors to
production and worldwide distribution.
This book is produced on FSC certified stock, within ISO14001
standards. The printer plants sufficient trees each year through
the Woodland Trust to absorb the level of emitted carbon in
its production.

The Wings of Isis

A temple by temple guide to The Magic and Ritual of Egypt

Lady Brenda McKoy

BOOKS

Winchester, UK
Washington, USA

CONTENTS

Introduction   vii

Part One: Entrance to the Temple   1
Chapter One: The History of Egyptian Magic
                 and the Isian Tradition   2
Chapter Two: The Egyptian Working Tools   20
Chapter Three: Temple Ethics   44

Part Two: The Inner Sanctum   65
Chapter Four: Isis and the Temple of Philae   66
Chapter Five: Osiris and the Temple of Abydos   89
Chapter Six: Horus and the Temple of Edfu   109
Chapter Seven: Hathor and the Temple of Dendera   128
Chapter Eight: Sekhemet and the Temple of Karnak   155
Chapter Nine: Bastet and the Temple of Tel Basta   170
Chapter Ten: Tehuti and the Great Pyramid   189

Journey's End   211

Footnotes   212

Bibliography   213

Introduction

What better way to begin our journey into the mysteries of Egyptian Magic and its rich history and practices than with the great temples of Egypt themselves. For contained in these temples or 'Houses of the Gods' is a microcosm of the Egyptian belief system in its entirety. A belief system, like many ancient belief systems, that was built upon the laws of nature and the universe.

These were my thoughts as the inspiration for this book unfolded. Revealed to me not so coincidentally, in the inner sanctum of the Temple of Isis as myself and my student travelers were gathered around the stone altar. As I invoked the goddess Isis, I could feel the temple awaken and vibrate with the magic and ritual of thousands of years. This was what the ancients had spoken of as the 'Hikau', or Life Force, the intangible energy that they accepted as a gift from the divine Creator, mother/father to the gods and goddesses. A Life Force that lived within all living beings, that vibrated from nature and the universe and was to them the source of all magic. The temples stood not only as vessels for the gods and goddesses but they housed their specific attributes and the 'Hikau' as well.

As a practitioner connecting the rituals of the gods with the temples gave me a sense of completion, of coming home, the spiritual home of Egyptian Magic and the Isian Tradition. For it was in the temples that the people of Egypt, pharaohs and commoners alike, met and communed with their gods and participated in festivals and rituals to the specific deities throughout the year.

Every step that I took upon those ancient stones spoke to me that day, inspiring me to create a tactile approach to the mysteries of Egyptian Magic. I realized that I could not bring the temples and my experiences back with me. I also realized that my practice of Egyptian Magic and the Isian Tradition would not be complete without including the history, traditions and the rituals of these great temples. For how can ones magical knowledge be complete without first walking upon a path that the gods themselves trod? In recreating the rituals and ceremonies of the temples in the great temples themselves, it is my hope that this book shall serve as a spiritual travel guide for the Egyptian magical practices of today shedding a light on the origins of the gods and goddesses and their magical attributes.

Contained herein are a collection of authentic Egyptian rituals, spells, amulets, and meditations. Some of the sources are taken from ancient papyri, some passed down through the underground priesthood, and some are a blend of tradition and our modern environment. They involve both the principles of High magic and Low magic and serve to open the way to connect us with the 'Hikau'. That magical source that is available to all of us who seek it and which is the very foundation stone of the Egyptian magical practices and the Egyptian religion. A compelling legacy that has not failed to fascinate all who had come in contact with it and one that has become the forerunner of many of the religions and spiritual practices that we know today.

Our journey begins with the basic nuts and bolts of the Egyptian magical practices, laid out like the temples themselves. Beginning with the Entrance to the Temple, the history, mythology, Gods and Goddesses, temple practices and the magical tools. The next section, the Inner Sanctum details the individual history and rituals that were performed in the main temples at the specific times of the year and the gods and goddesses that ruled them.

Interspersed throughout each chapter are the detailed notes from my travel journals so that this journey into the mysteries of Egyptian magic and the Isian Tradition may be seen and felt as well.

Anxs Uta Senb
Life, Health, Strength

~

Part 1
Entrance to the Temple

~

Chapter One

The History of Egyptian Magic and the Isian Tradition

To understand the practice of Egyptian Magic is to first understand the magical society that was ancient Egypt. A society where rituals and magic were intertwined with the peoples daily activities on all levels. A place where the gods and goddesses were seen not just as lofty figures but as real beings that participated in their lives.

Egyptian Magic and the Egyptian religion begins with the concept of the 'Hikau' an intangible, supernatural force that was present in both nature and the universe. This life- force called 'Hikau', was the essence that emanated from the Creator and the seed that brought all things into being. It could be felt and accessed by everyone from the Gods/Neters to priestesses and peasants, a force that permeated all levels of consciousness and that served the living as well as the deceased.

As in most ancient cultures the land and the sky were seen as the source of sustenance. In ancient Egypt the river Nile was seen as that source of all life, from birth to death and even into the afterlife. The Creator was to the people a spiritual form of the Nile.

The Creator was seen as both male and female and the gods and goddesses themselves were the male and female aspects of this One Creator force. A philosophy went on to baffle Egyptologists and practitioners alike for hundreds of years: For it posed the question of Monotheism, the belief in one central god, versus Polytheism, the belief in many gods and goddesses. At one time in Egypt's long history there were 6000 different individual gods and goddesses recorded.

The Creator provided all things like the river Nile. But to navigate the river one must be provided with a boat. Splendid, magical boats that could be seen in the form of gods and goddesses that were in tune with the rhythms of nature and the universe, and who could be appealed to directly by their mortal children.

Each god and goddess represented different concepts based on universal truths, also known as archetypes. Each archetype was identifiable with the physical, emotional and spiritual environment of Egypt and presented to its mortal children a means of direct communication with their gods in the form of ritual, magic and divination.

Throughout the long Egyptian history many different gods and goddesses gained and lost popularity. This was largely due to the power of the priesthood and the political climate at the time. Each dynasty had their popular group or pantheon of gods. Each province called a Nome and its villages had their own gods as well. While it may seem confusing, it made perfect sense to appeal to a local god for purposes related to your village and to appeal also to the Temple God for more lofty and serious things. Why is that? Because the Egyptians saw their deities as living beings not 'Pie in the Sky' untouchable concepts that ruled them with impersonal concern. These godlike beings actively participated in their lives, they were with them from birth to death and even guided them in the afterlife. To truly understand the Egyptian religion and its magical practices let us take a peek into the fascinating history of that great civilization.

The Chronology of the Egyptian Religion

The practices of Egyptian magic find their roots in the history of the Egyptian religion. This is especially true when we consider that magic, the 'Hikau', was intertwined with religion on all levels, from the humble altar of the peasant to the golden altars of the Temples. Over the thousands of years of Egyptian history the gods progressed side by side with their mortal children rising from the primitive pre-dynastic earth gods to the sophisticated celestial gods of healing and knowledge.

Pre-dynastic through Archaic Period
7000 B.C. through 2686 BC
Temples: Heliopolis and Abydos

The Pre-dynastic and Archaic period of Egyptian history is where the very roots of the Egyptian religion began. The primitive people of the time were hunter-gatherers who made their homes in mud huts beside the Nile. Their first concept of a mother goddess was Hathor, a goddess who in her most primitive aspect was seen as a cow, (most probably a water buffalo) and later as a woman with a cow's head. She represented fertility and sustenance, and her dark bovine hide was seen as the starry sky.

Alongside the mother goddess Hathor was her male counterpart the solar-warrior god, Horus. Represented as the falcon, whose attributes as a fierce warrior-hunter-protector were what the conflicted land of Egypt needed at that time. Pre-dynastic Egypt was a land torn by strife, a period when the northern and southern lands of Egypt were ruled by different kings. Horus became the patron deity of the Pharaohs' armies, a symbol of victory and remained so even after the two lands of Upper and Lower Egypt were united under the first dynasty.

During that time when the principle deities were Hathor and Horus, the main seat of Horus worship was located in the city of Heliopolis in Lower Egypt.

It was also during the first dynastic period that a mysterious event would occur that would alter the beliefs of ancient Egypt forever. That event was the arrival of a so called Master Race, foreigners that immigrated to the Nile Valley from an advanced civilization. They were called the Shemsu-Hor or the followers of

Horus. Their names were Tehuti, Osiris and Isis and they brought with them the knowledge of writing, medicine and planting crops.

Osiris, originally thought to be a mortal man, was crowned the first king of Egypt. He became deified through his deeds as a god of the people. Isis was crowned as his wife and queen becoming a goddess in her own right. Horus then became the personification of the Pharaoh, ever vigilant, whose strength and prowess stood as a mighty warrior for the people. The Cult of Horus and the Cult of Osiris existed side by side.

The principle temples of this period were located in Abydos and Heliopolis, and their groups of gods were called the Enead of Heliopolis. Writing and mathematics were introduced at this time along with the Pharonic Calendar. The Heb-Sed festival was created around the Osirian myth whereby the Pharaoh would seek to renew his reign by raising the Djed pillar, a symbol of fertility and an attribute that was associated with the death and resurrection of Osiris.

Old Kingdom
2686 BC through 2181 BC
Temples: Memphis and Abydos

The Cult of Osiris continued prominently in Abydos while a new group of gods, the Memphis Triad was born in the city of Memphis. It was at this time also that the the great Necropolis of Sakkara was designed and built by the infamous architect, Imhotep. Sakkara was destined to become the primary site of the pharoah's Heb-Sed festival. The Old Kingdom was the beginning of solar worship and pyramid building. Many of the pyramids of the Old Kingdom were patterned after the great pyramids at Giza. The esoteric perfection of the great pyramids though could never successfully be duplicated. The pyramids of the Old Kingdom, unlike the Giza pyramids, were built as tombs for the pharaohs. Their shapes designed to be an imitation of the rays of the Sun god Ra.

Meanwhile, during the 5th dynasty of the Old Kingdom, a humble, local goddess of Lower Egypt, Bastet, the cat goddess, began to rise in popularity in the Delta City of Bubastis.

First Intermediate Period
2181 BC through 2133 BC
Temples: Memphis and Abydos

The 7th through 10th dynasties were periods of unrest and political strife. Through this strife new religious doctrines were formed. One of these was called the 'Doctrine of the Ba' a treatise on the spiritual-karmic soul of a person, (the Ba), and its passage through the underworld. The Doctrine of the Ba led to the concept of the Judgement of the Dead. A ceremony in which Tehuti the God of Karma would weigh the heart of the deceased against a feather to see if it was pure enough to enter the afterlife. Coffin Texts, compiled by the priesthood called 'The Book of the Dead' were created at this time. The Book of the Dead contained prayers and spells that could be recited to aid the deceased in their passage into the afterlife. Through this text Osiris became well established as the underworld god of the Dead.

Middle Kingdom
2133 BC through 1786 BC
Temple: Thebes/Luxor

The Great Temple of Luxor was to become the religious center of Egypt in the 11th dynasty. A local god by the name of Amon-Ra rose to the status of Pharonic god. Amon-Ra along with Mut and Khonsu, formed the Thebian Triad. The Cult of Isis at this time began spreading in popularity among the people; and the Hyksos invaded the Delta bringing with them a mystical animal, the horse, which had never been found in Egypt, and a foreign god of rain and thunderstorms, Baal.

Second Intermediate Period
1786 BC through 1567 BC
Temple: Avaris

The 13th through 18th dynasties fell victim to the Hyksos. With this invasion arrived the Syrian gods. Syrian gods merged and morphed with the Egyptian gods. The Egyptian Set became equated with the primary Syrian god Baal. The Egyptian religion was eventually forced underground where it flourished in secret.

New Kingdom
1567 BC through 1085 BC
Temple: Thebes/Luxor, Amarna

The dawning of the New Kingdom at the end of the 18th dynasty saw Amon-Ra become a national god. Isis gained steadily in popularity and was declared the 'Queen of Heaven'.

Hatshepsut became the first female pharaoh and was to rule Egypt in peace, for 20 years. The next significant Pharaoh, the ruler of 'The Amarna period' was Amenhotep. Amenhotep became known as the 'Heretic' king. He changed his name to Akhenaten and created a monotheistic religion called Atenism. His religion was not well received by the priesthood or the people for that matter and therefore died out with his successor, the boy king Tutankhamun.

In the 19th dynasty Ramesses II took the throne and began massive building and rebuilding of the temples throughout Egypt, including Bubastis and Abydos. A traditionalist, Ramesses brought back many of the old gods of the Heliopolian Enead.

Late Period Transition
1085 B.C. through 656 BC
Temples: Tanis and Bubastis

Isis and her aspects of Bastet and Hathor gained in popularity during this period among the common people especially in Lower Egypt. In Luxor, Amon remains the principle god of the priesthood.

Late Period
664 BC through 332 BC
Temple: Bubastis, Philae

The Cult of Isis, the predecessor of the Isian tradition, becomes stronger with its principle temple located on the Island of Philae in Upper Egypt. Her feline aspect Bastet rules in the Delta. Alexander the Great conquers Egypt, and under Hellenistic influence Osiris merges with the sacred Apis bull to become the god Serapis.

Ptolomaic Period
332 B.C. through 32 BC
Temples: Philae, Edfu, Dendera

The Cult of Isis becomes the principal belief system led by none other than Cleopatra VII, who saw herself as a living representative of Isis on earth. During her reign Cleopatra VII built beautiful temples to Isis and Hathor throughout Egypt. Some of the best preserved of those temples can be seen today at Dendera and Philae.

The Roman Occupation
0 B.C. to 190 A.D.

After the defeat of the Egyptian fleet in Actium, Cleopatra and Antony commit suicide and the Romans seize what is left of the Egyptian Empire. Rather than dying out, the Egyptian religion is embraced by the Roman emperors who ironically have their names carved into cartouches to honor the Egyptian gods.

Isis and her cult become the darlings of Rome spreading to the shores of Italy and throughout the Mediterranean. The Osirian cult spreads throughout the West and to Rome as well.

In 54 A.D. Nero restores many of the temples and explores the source of the Nile, in 98 A.D. to 117 A.D. Trajan reactivates the ancient canal that leads from Bubastis to the Red Sea. Lastly, Hadrian founds the city of Antinoe in 117 A.D. to 190 A.D. The Egyptian religion and what is left of the priesthood go underground to surface again under the façade of the Copts. The Cult of Isis and Isis worship spreads across Europe.

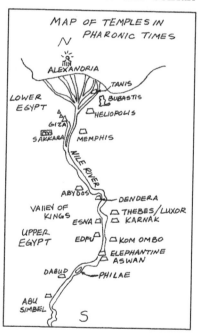

The Egyptian Pantheons
Unraveling the order of Egyptian deities has been quite a task for practitioners and Egyptologists alike, especially when you consider the fact that during the history of Egypt there have been over 6000 gods and goddesses recorded. These gods and goddesses can be separated into categories such as: Local gods,

Pharonic gods (which were available only to the Pharaohs), Animal gods, Temple Gods and Fetishes.

Gods of the Temples

The Enead of Heliopolis is the original group of deities whose archetypes were to shape the Egyptian Creation myth. This original myth was by far the oldest of the myths. It was altered many times throughout the various dynasties to keep up with whatever groups of gods were popular with the priesthood at the time. There were certain gods though that seemed to always be on top of their game, these cosmic celebrities were Ra, Horus, Osiris, Isis, Hathor, Bastet and Sekhemet.

The Enead of Heliopolis

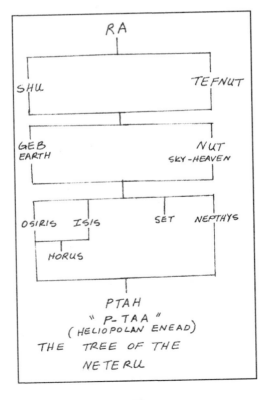

Tum

The Seed of Creation, Tum was the formless, indescribable force that existed within the universe. Tum could be felt on all planes of existence like the Hikau and was the force that animated the Divine Spirit of the Creator.

Ra-Atum

Known as 'He whose is complete in all things', Ra-Atum or Ra was the premiere god of creation, the Creator from which all things sprang into being. He represented the sun and its life giving solar rays. Ra was the father and grandfather of all the gods, who like the rays of the sun were the divine aspects of his creator force.

Shu

The god of air, Shu supported the sky; he represented the atmosphere, the air, which all living beings needed to survive. Shu embraced the earth, separating it from the sky. His name means to uphold, and he was shown in human form wearing a white feather headdress.

Tefnut

The wife of Shu, Tefnut was likened to the dew or moisture that nurtured the living things of the earth. Both sister and wife to Shu, she assisted in upholding the sky when the early morning sun (Ra) broke through her clouds in the east. Tefnut is often depicted in lion form or as a woman with a lion head much like the lion goddess, Sekhemet.

Geb

Geb was the God of earth and the father of Osiris, Isis, Nepthys and Set. All living things were said to be formed from his body. He was depicted in a human form with either black skin to represent the mud of the Nile or green skin for vegetation. On his head he wears the single crown of the south or the double crown of both north and south. His symbol is the goose and he ruled over agriculture and crops.

Nut

Nut is the goddess of the sky, the wife of Geb; she is most often depicted as supported by Shu, in the starry sky while arching gracefully over the earth. Her skin is blue and spangled with stars and was often depicted on the inside lid of the sarcophagus to watch over the deceased. Her children with the earth god Geb are: Osiris, Isis, Nepthys and Set.

Osiris

The God of the Underworld, Osiris was one of the immigrants from the land of the west. He was also the first king of Egypt. As a god of rebirth he ruled over crops and vegetation and was often depicted with ears of corn sprouting from his head. Osiris is shown as a green-skinned man wrapped in funerary bandages and was the first archetype of the mummy. As a man who became a god through suffering and death he was known as the Sacrificial Lord. He gave his life for the survival and stability of humankind.

Isis

The Queen of Heaven and the wife to Osiris, Isis was the goddess of magic and medicine. She was also the mother of the baby Horus whom she conceived of magically after the death of her husband Osiris at the hands of his jealous brother Set. Isis, whose name means throne, is depicted in human form with a horned, crescent crown on her head.

Set

The god of Chaos, Set was the antitheses of Osiris. While his brother was the god of resurrection and rebirth, Set was the god of destruction who found his home in the barren deserts in the south. Set conspired with evil conspirators to seize the crown of Egypt from his brother Osiris. Set is depicted as mysterious, long-snouted beast with square tipped ears, a species that is yet unknown or is most likely extinct.

Nepthys

The wife and sister of Set she presided over the edge of the desert, which could be either fruitful or barren. She was known as the Lady of the House and her symbol was the chalice headdress. Even through she was married to the evil Set she remained a devoted sister of Isis and assisted her in resurrecting her husband Osiris. Nepthys gave birth to Anubis the funerary god who turned out interestingly enough, to be none other than the illegitimate son of Osiris.

Horus

There were two representations of Horus that existed in the Myth of Creation and throughout the course of the Egyptian religion. They often times existed side by side and of were of course aspects of each other. They were Horus the Elder and Horus the Younger.

Horus the Elder was identified as far back as pre-dynastic Egypt as the God of the Sun. Horus the Younger was the son of Isis and Osiris, and went on to rule the land after the death of his father. Each Horus is depicted as a falcon or a falcon headed man. Horus the Elder often is seen to wear a sun disk on his head or two long feathers. Horus the younger was sometimes shown as a young boy wearing a braided side-lock of hair.

The Creation Myth

In the beginning, Tum, the Creator, spoke the sacred vowel of creation from his lofty disc of the sun. From this sacred vowel, came the seething waters of chaos, the primordial waters of Nu. Darkness and gloom covered the waters.

Out of the waters bloomed a red lotus blossom, from the center of her outspread petals a golden child appeared, he was the Sun God, Atum-Ra, and the radiance of his being shone out over the shadowy waters to banish the universal darkness.

However, the radiance of the young Sun God did not last. For each night the giant lotus would sink beneath the water and chaos would reign again. Each morning saw the young Sun God alone and solitary upon the lotus petals. He began to think what it would be like to have other beings to share this New World with him. So powerful were his thoughts that his mouth opened and he gave a great cry. As a result of that cry, the God of Air and the Goddess of moisture, Shu and Tefnut were born.

Shu and Tefnut fell in love with each other and in time they gave birth to twins, the Earth God Geb and the Sky Goddess Nut. So consuming was the love of Geb and Nut that for many years they embraced each other so tightly, the sky pressing against the earth, that nothing could grow between them. Their grandfather, Atum-Ra became jealous of the love they shared and ordered their father Shu to separate them. The mighty God of the Air trampled Geb beneath him, and then held Nut high above his head so that her husband could not reach her. Nut was pregnant but Shu put a curse on her so that she would not be able to give birth on any day of the year.

Nut leaned down towards her husband, but Shu, trapped by his father's strength could not reach her.

In the meantime Atum-Ra, the Creator had begun to give life to many other beings. One of the first of these beings was Tehuti or Thoth, the first High Priest of Egypt.

Tehuti looked up at the beautiful body of the Sky Goddess and he loved her, loved her and pitied her in her plight. He decided to help the unhappy goddess snd invented the game of draughts. He then challenged Atum-Ra to a game, where the stakes were to be time itself.

Skillfully, he managed to win enough time to make up five

days, as the length of the year in that time had been fixed to three hundred and sixty. The additional days won by Tehuti, did not fall into the days that were forbidden to Nut. At long last she was able to give birth to her children.

The first of Nut's children was born already crowned and his name was Osiris. On the second day Horus was born, then on the third day Set forced his way to earth through an open wound. The fourth and fifth day saw the birth of Isis and Nepthys.

The Memphis Triad

Ptah

During the first interme-
diate period of Egyptian
history, there were two
capitals, one for Upper
Egypt and one for Lower
Egypt. The capital city of
Lower Egypt was named
Memphis and it was the
home of a group of gods

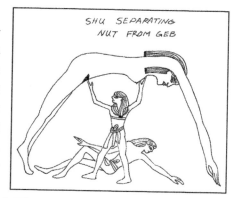

known as the Memphis Triad. These gods were very old in origin and were thought to have sprung separately from the primordial waters of Nu. The head of these gods was Ptah, an androgynous, Creation God, believed to be the Architect of the Universe. Under the command of Ra's brother Tehuti, he designed the heavens and the earth. More importantly he was a god that could be related to personally, on an earthly level. As a god of craftsmen, his skill in sculpting, casting and forging appealed directly to the populace. So strong was his following that when the Egyptian priesthood went underground for the last time during the roman occupation his cult flourished under the name of 'Freemasonry'. A belief system, that has survived to this day and can boast the membership of nearly all the founding fathers of the United States.

Sekhemet

The wife and consort of Ptah, Sekhemet was known as 'The Powerful' and was depicted as a lioness or a woman with a lioness' head. She was the goddess of war that embodied the fiery rays of the sun. Sehkemet was also the patron goddess of surgeons and was almost always the recipient of blood or the so called wet sacrifices.

Nefertem/Imhotep

The son of Ptah and Sekhemet, Nefertem was the god of healing. Known as 'He who comes in peace' he brought the art of healing to the people. During the Old Kingdom Nefertem merged with the deified Imhotep, the famous architect of the step pyramid at Zozer, located in the necropolis of Sakkara and also the temple of Abydos.

The Thebian Triad

Amon

In the 11th dynasty during the Middle kingdom, a local god by the name of Amon rose to become the premiere god of the Thebian priesthood. His archetype was that of an all-powerful and all knowing god of regeneration and reproduction, combining the highest powers of Ra and Osiris. The Cult of Amon eventually merged with the archaic Cult of Ra. Some of the most powerful women in ancient Egypt were priestesses of the Cult of Amon and were known as: the 'Wives of Amon'. These priestesses had political powers equal to the priests and often changed the course of government. Priestesses of Amon could only be appointed by their predecessors; a new priestess could only come into power if she was adopted by a former priestess before her death.

Mut

Mut was the sky goddess and the wife of Amon. Her name means 'Mother' and she is depicted as a vulture with wings outspread, or a woman wearing a vulture headdress. Images of Mut are often seen gracing the very top lintels of the temple doorways. She was revered for her ability to transform death into the living, much like the vulture feeds upon the dead to promote life.

Khonsu

The god of the moon, Khonsu appears in human form with a crescent headdress. Known as 'He who crosses the sky in a boat' he was associated with traveling and navigation. His later aspects became one of a messenger. Eventually, his archetype appeared to merge with that of Tehuti so that he was referred to as Khonsu-Tehuti , the 'Twice Great'. His lunar attributes were said to directly affect women and their fertility, therefore making him a god of fertility and reproduction. A very mysterious god, he

embodied many of the magical traits of Tehuti, so much so that he was called upon for healing and exorcisms.

The Isian Traditon

Isis and the Isian Tradition have been in existence from the very beginning of Egyptian history. From the first dynasties, where her archetype, the mother goddess blended with the pre-dynastic Hathor. Isis' position as supreme mother goddess gained even more validity through the Osirian Myth and the rise of the Cult of Osiris. Here she was seen not only as an earthly mother goddess but also as a divine sorceress who could perform magical healings. Isis and Osiris were viewed as a divine pair, part of the Enead of Heliopolis. It was not until the priesthood seized control of Thebes that she was recognized separately from her divine spouse.

The Isian tradition, a.k.a. the Cult of Isis, made its debut around 2000 B.C. when Thebes became the capital and religious center of Egypt. The foundations of the 'Mysteries of Isis' placed her as the central figure, rather than Osiris or the androgynous Ptah. The priesthood did this for two reasons: one, so that they would return to basics and the mother-goddess concept, and secondly, they feared invasion from foreign gods, namely the Babylonian Ashtoreth.

The Cult of Isis was formed to protect the image of Isis as the wife and mother of their God and therefore of the land of Egypt itself.

During the post-Alexandrian period, the pharaoh Ptolomy I was called upon by the priesthood to systemize the ideology of the Egyptian religion. For this task he appointed two men, Menetho the Egyptian priest and historian and a Greek named

Timotheus.

Their research led them to the very beginnings of the Cult of Isis: To the pre-dynastic period where she established herself as a 'Great Sorceress' who rose in the sky with the Sirius Star and whose magical abilities set her aside from just the mother goddess image. For not only could Isis give birth and procreate, but through magic, she could manipulate fate and bring the dead back to life.

The Ptolomaic society saw her as a goddess of all things and this faith was to eventually eternalize her as a goddess for all time. So strong was her following that instead of being ground underfoot by the Roman war machine she invaded the very shores of Italy. Magnificent temples were built in her honor and Roman citizens prostrated themselves upon their steps.

From Rome, the Cult of Isis spread across Europe. During the Christian era, she went underground, sometimes assuming the form of the Virgin Mary. In the twentieth century there was a revival of the Mysteries of Isis, led by the controversial medium Madame Blavatsky. In the 1970s, Isian groups were starting to come out into the light, chief among these the Fellowship of Isis.

Today the Isian tradition lives on in groups and organizations all over the world. Their practices are devoted to preserving the lore and ritual of the Isian Tradition which include:

- Herbalism and Healing Arts
- The Doctrine of the Right and True, (the belief in karmic balance and judgment)
- The Practice of Magic, Spellwork and Divination
- The belief in Resurrection and Immortality
- Contribution to the Ecology of the Earth
- Archiving of ancient writings and languages
- Respect for the hierarchy of the priestess

Chapter Two

The Egyptian Working Tools

When I first embarked upon my Egyptian spiritual path, I remember that one of the most fascinating aspects of that tradition were the magical workings tools. Strange and exotic to behold, these magical tools, I felt, in many ways were keys to the Egyptian magical philosophy.

I could not wait to start working with them! I was disappointed, however, to discover that they were nearly impossible to find. I had to make nearly all of them by hand. An experience that proved to be not only rewarding, but one that added personal power to my tools as well.

Each tool, as with all magical occult tools, represented esoteric concepts. Universal truths, that existed in nature and the universe. The tools themselves, became focal points to harness and manipulate these same universal forces. In turn the tools become the instruments in which to focus a person's will.

As ritual tools, they become a part of the user's energies and once consecrated they must never be used or touched by anyone other than the owner of the tools.

The origins and history of the Egyptian working tools are  just as mysterious and obscure as ancient Egypt itself. Some of the tools represent elements of creation, others represent magical concepts, while others still, are the personal tools used in working with specific deities.

The Ankh

Element: Fire
Deity: Tehuti, Atum Ra, Sekhemet, and Osiris
Association: South

The Ankh or Ankus, is definitely the most well known of all the Egyptian working tools, and like its symbol, it has possessed an almost eternal popularity throughout the ages. The symbol of the Ankh, sometimes called the cross of Tehuti, is a composite symbol and almost certainly the predecessor of the Celtic and Coptic Christian cross. It represents the Life Force, creation, God, his sacred word and the primordial waters of Nu (waters of creation). The origins of the Ankh are said to be Atlantean, introduced to the land of Egypt with Tehuti, the Divine Scribe and first High Priest of Egypt when he emigrated from the Land of The West, Atlantis.

Traditionally the Ankh was made of solid, pure gold or an orange gold called orichalum, an ore that was only mined in ancient times. As pure gold would be quite impossible to attain in this day and age, your personal Ankh can be made of copper, bronze, brass, wood and even self-hardening clay.

Your personal Ankh should be between 12 and 18 inches long with a loop and handle that is equally balanced.

The Ankh is a tool of fire. It embodies the life-force or Sekhem and was used by the Egyptian priests to give the 'Breath of Life' during magical ceremony. Your Ankh is the most personal and important of your magical tools and can be likened to the Wiccan Athame or ritual knife and as such, is used as an extension of the practitioners will and life force.

Construction of your Ankh

Perhaps one of the easiest ways to construct your Ankh is from copper tubing. Copper tubing can be found in the plumbing section of your local hardware store and is a soft metal that is easy to manipulate. Copper is also a magical metal and a powerful conductor of energy as well.

What you will need:

Copper tubing ½″ in diameter
Copper wire
1 rubber or wooden mallet
Small hacksaw
Gold metallic paint

Begin by first bending your copper into a large loop at one end, 6 to 9 inches long. Then make the handle piece of equal length. With your hacksaw cut off the crossbar at approximately 9″.

   With your mallet beat the crossbar piece as flat as you can. When you have reached a desired flatness attach the crossbar to the loop and handle by wrapping it tightly with the copper wire.

   When that is done, your Ankh is completed, you can choose to either keep it the natural copper or spray-paint it gold.

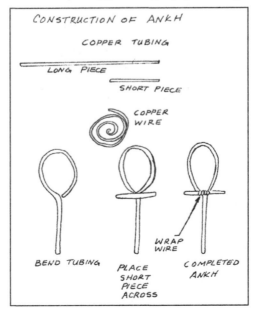

The Sistrum

Element: Air
Deity: Hathor, Bastet and Isis
Association: East

Like the Ankh, the Sistrum, or rattle is also one of your most important working tools. The Sistrum symbolizes the expression of harmony between the female and male principles, and a divine blending of the two energies.

The history of the Sistrum can be traced back to the Old Kingdom and the worship of the pre-dynastic cow goddess Hathor. At that time during the Old Kingdom, the appearance of the Sistrum was actually Hathor headed and was mounted on a Naos, a small shrine which resembled the horns of the goddess. Later, the Sistrum took on an Ankh-like shape in which the oval-shaped loop was surmounted by the cat goddess Bastet, one of the primary goddesses along with Hathor and Isis that was associated with the Sistrum. One myth suggests that the Sistrum was given as a gift to Bastet from her Divine Mother, Isis.

Writings from ancient texts describe blessings that were sung as songs and that were accompanied by the Sistrum. As a magical instrument, each of the four cross bars of the Sistrum represented an element of creation, air, fire, water and earth and their corresponding musical note. The four bars were thought to have been originally strummed rather than shaken.

As a magical tool, the Sistrum is used in purification and invocation, to dispel negativity and send out the 'Hikau' or words of power.

Construction of your Sistrum:

I have had great luck with two types of materials when constructing my Sistrums. Copper strips and self-hardening clay. The sturdier of the two being of course the copper while smaller, more personal, altar Sistrums work fine made out of clay.

Copper Sistrum

What you will need:

Copper strip 1 ½" wide
Copper, brass, or nickel-plated wire
Cymbals or small coin-sized discs
1 unpainted, decorative wooden table leg approx. 10" to 12" in length
1 bolt and screw
Drill or Screw gun
Wire cutters

To begin constructing your Sistrum, start by first bending the copper strip to form an oval shape. It should be the equal length of your wooden table leg. Bend the ends of the oval flat and then drill a hole through the middle. Attach the oval to the wooden

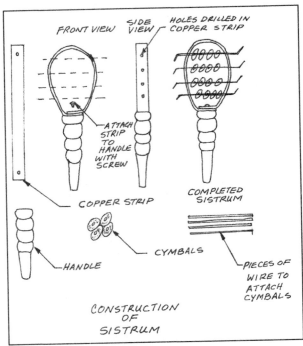

FRONT VIEW   SIDE VIEW   HOLES DRILLED IN COPPER STRIP

ATTACH STRIP TO HANDLE WITH SCREW

COPPER STRIP

COMPLETED SISTRUM

HANDLE

CYMBALS

PIECES OF WIRE TO ATTACH CYMBALS

CONSTRUCTION OF SISTRUM

table leg with the bolt and screw. When the oval is attached firmly to the handle measure your wire so that each piece of wire is equal and has 1" extra on either side of the loop. Measure the hole- spaces evenly on both sides of the loop then drill your holes. When your holes are drilled, place one wire at a time through one side of the loop. String the cymbals onto the wire. The amount of cymbals will vary with the size of the loop but there never should be less than five. When you have finished stringing the cymbals, crimp or curl the ends of the wire on both sides.

You can now decorate your Sistrum by painting the handle either gold or a celestial blue. Cat figurines or a Hathor head can be added to the top as well as braided or beaded ropes added to decorate the handle.

Clay Sistrum

What you will need:
Self-hardening or Fimo clay
Thin copper wire
Cymbals or small coin shaped discs
Awl

In constructing your clay sistrum you have an opportunity to get really creative. Keep in mind though, that your clay Sistrum should not be more than 9" long to prevent breakage.

Begin by forming the loop and handle of your Sistrum making it either flat or rounded. Attach the two pieces with a crossbar.

Using your Awl, make four sets of holes for the wire. Decorate your Sistrum by pressing Egyptian symbols or jewelry into the clay. If you are really artistic you can form a small cat or Hathor figure for the top. Bake your clay in the oven for the recommended time.

When it is done remove it from the oven to cool completely. After it has cooled attach the cymbals by stringing them on the wire. Tie off or crimp the end of your wire. When that is done you can paint you Sistrum metallic gold, copper, or celestial blue.

The Winged Disk
Element: Air/Spirit
Deity: Horus
Association: East

The Winged Disk is another one of the tools that possesses other-wordly origins. One interpretation is that it stems from an ancient concept of Heaven. A concept that represents heaven as a solar disk flanked on either side by wings. The wings being indicative of the wings of a falcon stretched over the world. Another, more esoteric meaning and one that is used in magical practices is of the winged disk representing concept of time through space, or time travel.

The symbol of the Winged Disk has appeared in Egyptian art as far back as the 5th dynasty where it began as a pair of wings supporting the solar barque in which Horus the falcon rode. The original deity associated with the Winged Disk was the god Behdet 'He with the colored plumage'. Behdet was later replaced by the Celestial Falcon Horus, who merged with Behdet to become the symbol kingship. At the end of the Old Kingdom the Winged Disk acquired two Uraei (divine serpents) on either side of the disk. They symbolized the eyes of Ra and the upper and lower kingdoms of Egypt and were even shown with their respective crowns.

By the time of the Middle Kingdom the symbol of the Winged Disk was carved above the doorways of temples for protection. In the ritual space, the Winged Disk is hung above the altar facing east, it is also used during astral travel to guide a persons Ka back to his or her body. Amulets of the Winged Disk are used for protection in this life and the next.

Construction of the Winged Disk

Your Winged Disk can be made of various materials: Wood, thin sheet metal, clay and stained glass. The clay method however, is by far the easiest.

What you will need:

Self- hardening clay or Fimo clay
Butter knife
Awl
Rolling pin
Various paints: Red, Blue, gold and black

Start by rolling your clay out flat, about ¼" thick using the rolling pin. Using the following pattern cut out the outline of your Winged Disk. Place it in the oven for the appropriate time. When it is done take it out and let it cool. Paint your Disk starting with red for the center and blue and gold for the rest, using the black to outline the disk and the wings.

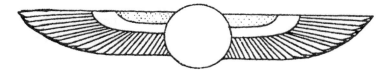

The Crook and Flail

Deity: Osiris
Association: North, South

This famous Egyptian symbol has been identified as emblem of the Pharaohs from time immemorial. The most famous example of this tool is the gold and lapis lazuli Crook and Flail that lies across the breast of the sarcophagus of Tutankhamon.

This symbol, that has been associated with kingship and sovereignty, has many deeper, esoteric meanings as well. Held in the hands of the king, who was himself, a magical adept, it stood

for balance, justice and fertility. The Crook referred to as the Hekat, represents the 'seed', action and ferment and can possibly be identified with the shepherd's crook of the pre-dynastic god Anedjiti 'the Chief of the Eastern Nome'. The Flail, the Nekhakha, a shepherd's whip from the same god, represents physically expressed energy.

The Crook/Hekat is held in the left hand, the receiving hand of the north, the *above*. The Flail/Nekhakha is held in the right hand, the south, the side that restores and gives, the *below*.

Used in ritual, these two symbols channel the Sekhem energy through the body. The flail can also be brushed lightly over a person to activate their Life Force.

Construction of the Crook and Flail

Traditionally, the Crook and Flail was made of wood covered in pure gold and inlaid with lapis lazuli. Today's practitioners make theirs out of either wooden dowels or copper tubing. The copper tubing method is by far the easiest and adds the extra bonus of being a great conductor of energy.

What you will need:

½" copper tubing
Copper wire
Gold and blue beads
Gold and celestial blue, enamel spray paint that is suitable for metal
1" thick masking tape
1 small hacksaw

Your personal Crook and Flail must be equal in length. The measurement should be the distance from your middle finger to your elbow, 1 cubit.

Begin construction your Crook and Flail by first by bending the tubing into a crook shape. Cut off the bottom with the hacksaw. Do the same with the Flail piece. Place the two pieces on newspaper and spray paint them in the metallic gold. When the paint is completely dry, tape off one-inch sections on both pieces using the masking tape. Spray paint the two pieces again, this time with the celestial blue.

When that paint is completely dry, carefully remove the tape. Your Crook and Flail should be a beautiful gold and blue. Drill two small holes at the top of the Flail and add a small loop of the copper wire. Attach three short pieces of wire to that loop, approximately seven inches long. String the beads in an alternating pattern onto the copper wires. When you are done the Flail ends should swing freely.

Lotus Bowl and Sacred Vessel
Element: Water
Deity: Nepthys
Association: West

The Sacred Vessel or Chalice is the symbol of the underworld goddess Nepthys. It represents the element water, the fluid of Birth and the Blood of the Mother. The Chalice of Nepthys, much like the cauldron of the Celtic goddess Cerridwen holds the fluids of rebirth and transformation. On the Egyptian altar, the Sacred Vessel is used for scrying and ritual libations of either wine or beer. It should be made of a clear green or blue glass.

LOTUS
BOWL

Lotus Bowl

The Lotus Bowl, just by virtue of being lotus-shaped, puts one in mind of creation myth where the birth of the 'Divine Child' took place upon the lotus flower, in the primordial waters of Nu. It is a symbolic vessel of purification, with purification being naturally the first step in all magic ritual, thus for creation itself. Your Lotus Bowl holds the Natron water or salt water and is generally made of white porcelain or in some cases brass. Lotus Bowls can be acquired at specialty shops especially those who cater to Oriental cooking.

The Mirror of Hathor

Element: Earth
Deity: Hathor
Association: North

A sacred attribute of the goddess Hathor, the Hathor mirror has several uses in Egyptian magical practices. The mirror itself represents the element of earth and as such can be used in reflecting negative energies back to their sources, in affect, grounding them. The mirror is also used in protection rituals and for summoning the forces of earth, the animals, deities and low- level spirits associated with it.

As a divination tool, the Hathor Mirror can be used for scrying, much like a crystal ball or magic mirror. Traditionally, the Hathor Mirror was made of bronze with one side highly polished and the other side scoured to deflect negative energies.

How to construct your Hathor Mirror:

Perhaps the easiest way to make your Hathor Mirror is by using a copper disk with a wood or self-hardening clay handle. If you are really handy with metalworking your whole mirror can be constructed out of copper and copper strips. The following method is the one I find the most artistically rewarding.

What you will need:

Self–hardening clay or Fimo clay

1 copper disk approximately 5 to 6 inches in diameter

Model glue

Various paints

Copper polishing compound

Steel wool or wire brush

Begin constructing your mirror by first scouring one back of your copper disk with the steel wool or wire brush. When that is done, polish the other side with the polishing compound to the highest shine possible then set it aside.

Next, mold your clay into a Hathor-head shape, complete with curved horns and handle. When you are finished take up your disk and press it into the top of the Hathor handle making a small

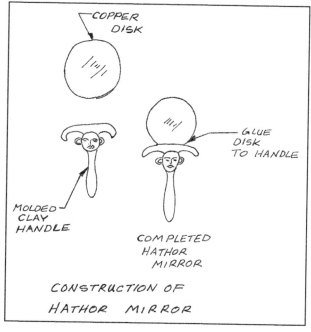

COPPER DISK

GLUE DISK TO HANDLE

MOLDED CLAY HANDLE

COMPLETED HATHOR MIRROR

CONSTRUCTION OF HATHOR MIRROR

groove approximately ¼" deep. Then bake your clay according to the directions.

When the clay is done remove it from the oven and let it cool completely. Paint it in the colors of your choosing. Finally, using the model glue, attach the disk to the top of the handle when it is dry your mirror is ready to use.

The Oil Lamp
Element: Fire
Deities: Spirit of the Lamp
Association: South

The magical, mysterious, Oil Lamp has a many and varied purpose in Egyptian magic. In its most basic form, it is used to represent the element fire on the altar. In its most esoteric, the Oil Lamp is the premier tool of divination in the Egyptian Tradition. The Leyden Papyrus alone contains dozens of ancient Oil Lamp divinations.

The Egyptians believed that there was a 'Spirit of the Lamp' much like the 'Genie of the Lamp' that could be invoked to answer questions and reveal the future.

Elaborate rituals were performed called 'Divination by Vessel' or Oil Lamp divination. Many times in these rituals, a priest or priestess would use a young child (under the age of puberty) to channel the Spirit of the Lamp. In magic and spell-work, the petitioner's desires were written on the wicks of the oil lamp. When the lamp was lit, their desires were ignited by the flames and rose into the heavens by way of the lamp smoke, so that they could be seen and acknowledged by the gods.

Traditional Oil Lamps from ancient Egypt came in many forms. They were cast in bronze, forged in copper and even formed in ceramic. The oil that was used for the lamps was a very refined, light oil, from the sacred olive tree.

The Oil Lamps that are available today are most often the Indian brass, genie lamps. You can also find museum replicas made out of bronze or clay. Before using your lamp, always make sure to check for any leaks, as they may become hazardous when the lamp is lit. The oil that is used today is simple, unscented lamp oil. I personally, have not been able to burn any of the olive oil available to me, with any success.

The Caduceus
Element: Spirit
Deity: Tehuti
Association: East

This famous symbol known as the Greek staff of healing, or the staff of Ascelepeus, has been an attribute of the medical profession for thousands of years. The Caduceus however, originated as a magical tool of the god Tehuti, whom the Greeks called Thoth.

The Caduceus is a wand surmounted by a winged disk about which two serpents are entwined. The two serpents represent the elements of fire and water. They are coiled about the staff three times making three loops, symbolizing the Earth, Heaven and the Duat (underworld). The serpents, symbolic of wisdom, cross over four times one for each element of creation. The Winged Disk represents the higher level of the spirit and the ability to traverse freely through that level.

Magically, the Caduceus is used like a wand, and becomes the extension of the user's higher mind or words.

Traditionally, the Caduceus was made of wood gilded with pure gold. These days your Caduceus can be made of either wood, brass, or self-hardening clay. Whatever you choose to make your Caduceus from, it will prove to be, by far, your most challenging tool to construct.

How to construct your Caduceus:

The easiest plan for the construction of your Caduceus, is one that uses both wood and self-hardening clay.

What you will need:

12" long 1" thick wooden dowel rod
Self-hardening clay or Fimo clay
Model glue
Various colored paints

Begin making your Caduceus by first painting the wooden dowel rod a metallic gold. Next roll the clay out into long thin cylinders

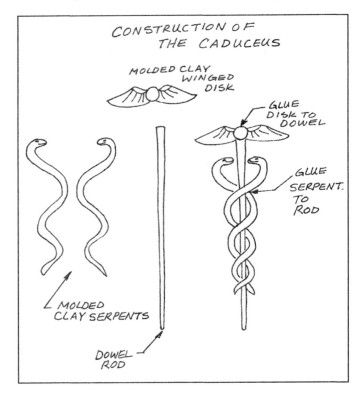

and form them into serpents to your best artistic ability. Wrap each serpent around the dowel three times as shown in the following illustration. Set them aside on a baking sheet. Then form the Winged Disk making sure to create a hole in the bottom so that it can fit onto the top of the dowel rod. Place the Winged Disk onto the baking sheet along with the serpents and bake them according to directions.

When the clay has finished baking and has sufficiently cooled, you can glue each piece on separately starting with the serpents first. When all the pieces are glued to the dowel rod you can finish your Caduceus by painting it. Gold paint is used for the Winged Disk, and green or blue for the serpents.

The Thurible

Element: Air
Association: East
Deity: Neith

The Thurible or incense burner has many and varied uses in Egyptian ritual. Shallow and bowl-like in appearance it is usually made of brass or bronze and is large enough to accom-  modate the burning of herbs, incense and offerings. In ancient times the Thuribles used in the temples were as large as braziers and were often placed on the floor. Smaller, decorative hand-held thuribles were used in invocation and to ritually cense a person or object. The smoke from your Thurible even though it is born from fire gives substance to the element air.

The Waset Scepter
Deity: Anubis

Perhaps one of the most mysterious of all the Egyptian tools, is the Waset or Was Scepter. This staff-like implement is an important tool of the High Priest and is awarded only after the highest degree of study has been accomplished. Strange to behold, it resembles a staff with a curved top and forked end. An animal head resembling a canine or composite creature is carved on the curved top.

In the early part of Egyptian history, this creature was thought to be a sort of fetish or protective, fox-like spirit. In Myth, the Waset Scepter, was said to have been placed in the hands of the Neters or gods as a divine attribute. It was referred to as the 'Vivifying Sap'or the 'Key to the Nile'. Purported to possess great healing and regenerative powers, it was often seen in the hands of gods, such as Osiris, Horus, Ptah and Amon.

In the Middle Kingdom, the Waset Scepter was placed in the tomb with the deceased so that he or she would enjoy divine prosperity. So important was this symbol, that a Nome from Thebes was named after it.

In magical practices the Waset Scepter is used in rituals of great healing, to align the seven spinal Chakras, or energy centers in the body, much like a giant tuning fork. The Waset is a conductor of the Sekhem or Life Force energy and can awaken and heal on all three levels, physical, emotional and spiritual. Traditionally, the Waset Scepter was made of a sacred wood, encased in gold. Later more modern versions were made of copper or solid brass.

How to construct you Waset Scepter:
The Waset Scepter is most easily constructed out of copper tubing, again from your local hardware store.

What you will need:

Copper tubing ¾" thick

Small hacksaw

Copper wire

Power Drill

Self-Hardening Clay or Fimo

Gold metallic paint

Hot glue gun

Begin the construction of your Waset Scepter by bending the copper tubing at the top into a small curve. Then carefully measure the length of your Waset. It should be shoulder height, with the curved top reaching your shoulder.

Using the hacksaw, cut off a piece of excess tubing approxi-

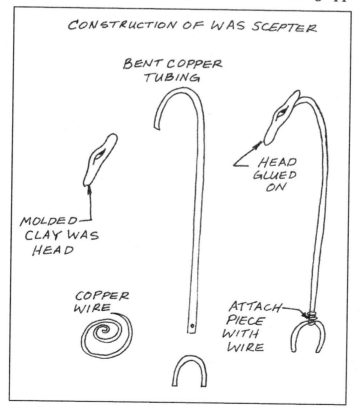

CONSTRUCTION OF WAS SCEPTER

BENT COPPER TUBING

HEAD GLUED ON

MOLDED CLAY WAS HEAD

COPPER WIRE

ATTACH PIECE WITH WIRE

mately 6" long. Bend that piece in to a sharp crescent shape and set aside.

Next mold the fox-like head of the Waset out of the clay, making sure to create a hole at the top the same diameter as the copper tubing, then bake it in the oven for the prescribed time.

Attach the crescent-shaped piece of tubing to the bottom of your staff by first drilling small holes through the tubing approximately ½" from the bottom. Then wrap the copper wire around the crescent shaped piece. Thread the wire through the holes and wrap it tightly.

Finally attach the fetish head to your Waset using a generous amount of hot glue. When the glue has set, you can spray paint the whole staff in metallic gold if desired.

The Lotus Scepter
Deities: Isis, Sekhemet

Where the Waset Scepter is the tool of the High Priest the Lotus Scepter is the tool of the High Priestess. It is always made from the wood of a fruit tree, either pomegranate, olive or orange. It is a symbol of the law and authority of the High Priestess coupled with the female principles of rebirth, regeneration and wisdom. Like the Waset Scepter, the Lotus Scepter is awarded upon the completion of the higher stages of magical studies.

Construction of your Lotus Scepter:
The most desirable way to make your Lotus Scepter would be to carve it entirely out of wood, as this is not always possible the next alternative is to use the wood of a fruit tree surmounted by a clay lotus flower.

What you will need:
1 shoulder high staff made out of a fruit wood
Self hardening clay or Fimo

Blue paint
Model glue
Reddish colored wood stain
To begin constructing your Lotus
Scepter we will start in the usual way
by molding a lotus flower out of the
clay to the best of our artistic ability.
Place the lotus flower in to the oven
and bake it according to directions.
When it is done attach the lotus to the
top of the staff using the model glue.
Paint the lotus blue and stain the staff
with a reddish colored wood stain.

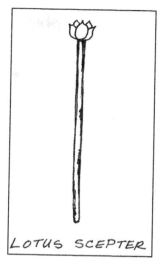

LOTUS SCEPTER

The Purification and Consecration of your working tools

As with any other magic tradition, your personal working tools as
well as your working space will need to be purified and consecrated before use. Purified first, to get rid off all negative energies
that may have attached themselves to them, and then followed by
a consecration to empower them with positive energies.

Your Sacred Space

Your Sacred Space will be the area in which you have designated
as your personal temple. It is here in this Sacred Space that all of
your magic and ritual will take place with the exception of rituals
performed outdoors. If you are lucky and have the luxury of a
separate room for your temple, that whole room will need to be
purified before any ritual is performed there. If you only have
part of a room or even just a corner of your bedroom, that space
will have to be as clean and as dust free as possible.

Purification must take place before each ritual to dispel any
negative energy that may have entered. You must be remember
that when you invoke the Gods/Neters you are opening portals
from other realms and these deities may react negatively to

hostile, unwanted energies.

Purification of your Sacred Space

The purification of your Sacred Space begins by first sprinkling the perimeters and corners with Natron water, starting in the east. Natron water is a solution of ½ cup of sea salt mixed with 3 tablespoons of bicarbonate of soda in purified water.

Follow up the Natron water by censing the corners with Frankincense, the perfume of Ra. As you do say these words:

"By the light and love of Amon Ra,
I purify this temple and consign back
Into the realms of the Abyss,
All that is impure, All that is evil and
All that is the enemy of the Right and True.
May all that is Maati flourish and may this
Sacred Space be clean to receive the Neters,
By the power of Amon Ra!
SE-HETEP-NUA NETER-EM MERT-F (I have appeased the gods by doing their will)"

The Ritual of Purification and Consecration of your Working Tools

Once your temple has been purified it is time to purify and consecrate your working tools. The ritual of purification needs to be during the waxing phase, over a period of seven days culminating on the full moon.

Ritual Checklist:

1 red candle
7 white candles
7 sacred oils: Lotus, Myrrh, Cedar, Frankincense, Sandalwood, Cassia oil, Balsam oil
Your working tools

Frankincense
Natron powder
Purified water
Red silk cloth
Wine and cakes for libation
Statue or picture of Isis, Osiris, Bastet or Horus
Ritual time: Waxing moon

Prepare for your ritual by taking a purification bath with your prepared Natron and nine drops of Myrrh oil. Relax in your bath and meditate on the golden light of Ra, let it enter your body driving out all the gray or dark areas. When you are done, dry off and dress in a clean, loose robe preferably the color white. Begin your ritual by first anointing the two candles, the red candle with the lotus oil and the white candle with the Cedar oil. Light both candles then the Frankincense. Cense all four corners with the Frankincense. Lay your working tools on the altar and sprinkle them lightly with the Natron water.

Raise your Sistrum to the east and shake it five times as you do say these words:

Hika,
Hika,
Hika,
Hika,
Hika,
I invoke thee O' great Neters of the Enead, Isis, Osiris, Bastet, Sekhemet, Horus and all the four sons of Horus, I seek your presence here in this temple, to add your Hikau (words of power)
To these magical tools of Art

Hold each tool up to the east then pass it through the Frankincense, when you are finished repeat these words:

Hail thee that ruleth the East Lord Duamutef
Jackal headed son of Horus, Neith warrior goddess,
Protectress, come forth from the Abyss to empower this tool
with the cleansing power of air

Then hold each tool up to the west and sprinkle it lightly with
purified water from altar, as you do so, say these words:

"Hail thou that ruleth the west, Lord Quebsenuf, falcon
headed son of Horus,
Selkit, scorpion goddess of magic come forth to empower this
tool with the transforming powers of water."

Next, hold each tool up to the north and sprinkle it lightly with
the Natron powder, as you do so, say these words:

"Hail thou that ruleth the north, Lord Hapi, ape headed son of
Horus, Nepthys, goddess of the underworld come forth from
the land of rebirth to empower this tool with the regenerative
power of earth."

Finally, hold each tool up to the south then pass it quickly through
the flame of the red candle as you do say these words:

"Hail thou that ruleth the south, Lord Imsety, human headed
son of Horus,
Sekhemet, lioness of the desert, guardian of the eternal flame,
come forth from the land of the Ureaus to cleanse this tool with
the Sekhem power of fire."

Your next step in your purification ritual will be to anoint each
tool with the seven sacred oils, one oil at a time, and one oil each
night.

Before you begin anointing take three deep 'Sekhem' breaths, fill your body with the golden light of Ra and envision that light entering each one of your tools. When you are done cover your tools with the red cloth until the next night. Snuff out the red candle and leave the white one to burn all the way down. Conclude your ritual with a libation of wine and cakes.

Repeat this ritual for the next six nights omitting the Natron purification at the beginning. On the seventh night, the night of the full moon, anoint your tools with the final oil. When you have finished do not cover them right away with the red cloth but allow them to absorb the power of the lunar light for a few hours. When this seven day process has been completed, your tools are now ready to be used.

ANKUS   UTA   SENB

Chapter three

Temple Ethics

As a magical society, ancient Egypt patterned its religious beliefs on a holistic system, one that worked in harmony with Universal Laws. It was based on a concept known as 'Maati', the Right and True. The system of Maati, was set forth by the first high priest of Egypt, Tehuti and it encompassed the concept of balance and harmony with nature and the universe. Maati was also the name given to the goddess Maat, a goddess of balance and justice who was the wife and consort of Tehuti himself. Maat presided over what was called the halls of Maati. These were the halls that the deceased must through pass to reach the place of judgment where his or her heart would be weighed against the red feather of Maat. If their heart was lighter that Maat's feather the deceased would be judged True of Heart and would be able to progress into the Afterlife. If the deceased heart proved to be too heavy, it would be devoured by a monstrous beast from the Abyss that was known as The Eater of Souls.

This concept of cosmic order and discipline is what immediately appealed to my Capricorn sense of balance and tradition. As a magical system it appeared to be not only rooted to the earth but stretching up to the heavens as well. This interconnection between humanity, the earth, and the universe was exactly what the sage Tehuti had meant by his words 'As Above, So Below'.

The law of cosmic order, a Karmic concept of cause and effect, was woven closely into the fabric of ancient Egyptian life on all levels. So much so, that the Egyptian people considered themselves connected to their gods as if they were indeed their earthly children. Egyptian magic and ritual was centered around communing with, and communicating with their gods. Invocation was performed to create a portal for their gods to enter the sacred space. These portals took the form of the great temples that were built according to the Egyptian's concept of the spiritual universe, the realm of the Neters, of which Egypt, referred to by the ancients as Kemet, was the reflection.

The following diagram shows the geography of Egypt and how it relates to the sacred temples and, in turn, to your own sacred space as well.

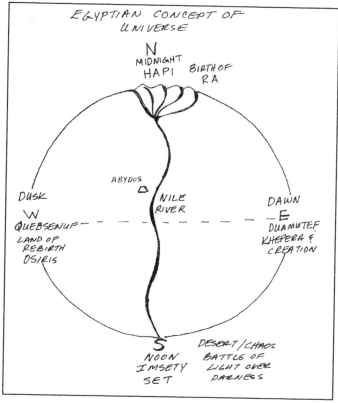

As you can see, the mouth of the River Nile is located in the northern most part of Egypt. The River Nile, the only river in the world that flows south to north, fans out into many tributaries as it meets the Mediterranean Sea in the North. These tributaries curiously resemble a Lotus flower. This symbolic lotus located in the northernmost direction of Egypt was the mythological birth-place of Ra.

Birthed at midnight, the first rays of the sun illuminated the Divine Sun Child Ra as he lay upon the open petals of the Lotus. Directly opposite him, the antithesis of the light and ruler of chaos, Set, the god that rules in the south, the barren desert which supports no life. The same desert in which Horus fought Set in the battle of light over darkness. In the west was Amenti, the realm of Osiris and the land of rebirth, the same direction in which the mummies were faced in their tombs. And finally, the east, the realm of Khepera the God of creation, from which all things spring to life anew.

Elemental Associations and the four sons of Horus

If you are familiar with the elemental associations of the western magical traditions, the Egyptian associations may at first seem a little confusing. Perhaps because there have been many schools of thought on the Egyptian elements and their associated deities, also known as the sons of Horus. Their tendency is to give the elements an association according to environment. In western magical practices, many traditions believe that the sun rising in the east brings renewal and the setting of the sun in the watery west brings rebirth after death. In the western hemisphere this is surely true. To those traditions, west and water are the elements of rebirth, and that is taken quite literally as a universal truth. The ancient Egyptians were a very earthy and literal people as well. They saw, as we mentioned previously the Spiritual Universe as consisting of the geography of Egypt known in the ancient world as Kemet, and all the various associated worlds of the Earth, Heaven and the Duat. These worlds encompassed a tri-leveled universe, which they believed defined the 'Temple on Earth' that was their land.

The East, the place of the dawn or rising sun was the realm of Khepera, Creation, and the element air. The West, symbolized

Earth and the place of the setting sun, the land of Osiris where the deceased would sink down into the underworld to be reborn. The North, the element water and midnight, was where the birth of Ra would take place. Finally, in the South, fire and noon represented the highest most destructive rays of the sun. The south was the home of Set and his fiery desert realm, the threshold to transformation and the place where the battle of light over darkness would take place.

Along with the elemental associations of the four cardinal points, the Egyptians had four corresponding deities called the Four Sons of Horus. These gods represented respectively the four elements of creation: Duamutef in the East, Imsety in the South, Quebsenuf in the West and Hapi in the North. Their father Horus, was the representation of the Creator on earth, and his sons represented the aspects of creation itself.

According to myth, the four sons of Horus were born from the goddess Isis and were to be the guardians and lords of the four pillars that supported the sky (the four elements). Their guardianship extended naturally to the organs of the physical body; thus, they are best known as the gods of the Canopic jars, which held the preserved organs of the mummy. Hapi the god of the North, protected the small intestines; Duamutef of the East, the lungs; Quebsenuf the god of the west, the liver and gall bladder and Imsety of the South, the stomach and large intestines.

According the Book of the Dead;

"The deceased is called their father. His two arms were identified with Hapi and Duamutef, and his two legs with Imsety and Quebsenuf, when he entered into the Seket-Aanru they accompanied him as guides, and went in with him two on each side. They took away all hunger and thirst from him, they gave him life in heaven and protected it when given"

Orientation of the Temple and Altar

Following naturally after the elemental associations is the orientation of the Temple or sacred space, then followed by the ritual altar. In the great temples, the sanctuaries and chapels are rectangular in shape. In the following illustration we can see a diagram of an Egyptian temple, which can serve as a model for your own sacred space. Notice that representations of the four elements are placed in each corner. A bowl of water for the North, The Winged Disk for the east, an incense thurible for the south and either a bowl of earth or a polished copper disk for the element earth in the West.

These symbols are separate from your working tools, and they

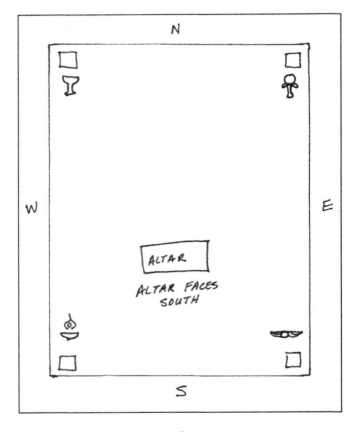

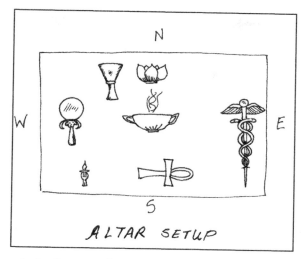

ALTAR SETUP

must remain in the sacred space at all times. Your altar should be set up facing the south, the direction of transformation. The tools are placed according to the illustration. You may add to it a statue or picture of your deity along with fresh flowers and small vessels to contain oil and Natron.

The Realms of the Other Worlds

The ancient Egyptians believed in the existence of Other Worlds where the deceased would travel upon his or her death. These other worlds were in the form of mythical realms, much like the concept of different dimensions. They conceived these realms to be existent on three spiritual levels, the Earth, Heaven and the Duat (underworld). Their belief was that the soul of a person was able to travel from realm to realm and meet with the deities that resided in them. Sometimes these sacred Other Worlds were even located in the temples themselves.

Abtu/Abydos

Abtu or Abydos, called Per-Ausar (the house of Osiris) was the capital of the eighth Nome of Egypt and the first religious center for the cult of Osiris. It was believed that when the sun set in

Abydos, a gap in the mountains opened into the Duat, and the souls of the dead would travel through this gap by means of an underground river. Here the deceased would be met by Osiris the God of the Dead and he would show them the way to the Elysian Fields, the Egyptian concept of paradise.

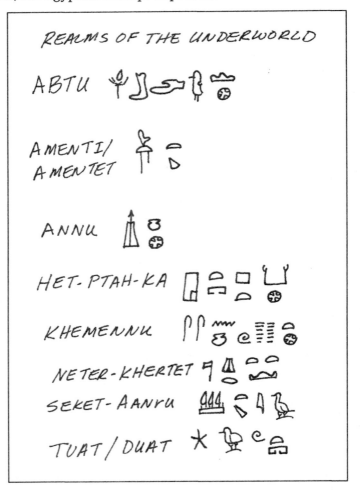

Amenti/Amentet

Amenti was thought to be at one time a funerary district in an actual town. Amenti was also the place where the dead awaited in their tombs to be reborn again. In places such as the Valley of the Kings the deceased, tombs were hewn out of the western facing mountains.

Annu

Annu, a city known to the Egyptians as Per-Ra (house of Ra) was another place that gained mythological notoriety. In pre-dynastic times it was a center for sun worship and the abode of 'The Old One', a form of Osiris and most specifically the 'Eye' of Osiris. It was here that the deceased were joined with thousands of other souls to be blessed, and to live on celestial food forever.

Het-Ptah-Ka

This was the sacred name given to the city of Memphis; it translates to 'House of the Ka of Ptah'. It was believed that the Ka of the creator god Ptah dwelled within this city during the first dynasties.

Khemennu

Located in the fifteenth Nome of Egypt, Khemennu was the abode of the eight great cosmic gods of the Ogdoad.

Neter-Khertet

Another name for the abode of the dead which translates as; 'The Divine Subterranean Place'.

Sekhet-Aanru

Here is a truly mysterious place, located in the Delta where the god Osiris would bestow fabulous estates on the souls of the dead so that they might live out their days feasting on every type of food in abundance.

Tuat/Duat

This is the infamous name for the underworld abode of the

deceased, a place were they would reside before entering the Afterlife. Located in the west, it also represents the subconscious plane of existence.

The Aspects of the Soul

The ancient Egyptians believed that the soul of a person or an animal had nine distinct aspects. This can be hard to conceive of when most people these days have a difficult time believing in one!

These nine aspects defined the spiritual body of a being by allowing it to move freely between the world of the conscious and unconscious worlds and, therefore, through all the planes of existences. Knowledge and use of these aspects were used extensively, not only the ritual of the temple, but in everyday magic as well.

Khat

The Khat is the physical body, or vessel, in which the soul was held. The Khat also refers to the mummified body, which became the symbolic vessel that held the eternal soul. During the mummification process this body was preserved against decay so that it would be whole in the afterlife.

Sahu

The Sahu, after undergoing the ritual of mummification became the vessel for the spiritual body. This ritual would act as a sort of initiation in which the physical body attained special knowledge and power which rendered it incorruptible in the Afterlife. The Sahu then allowed the soul to communicate with the body freely in the realms of heaven.

Ab

The Ab is the spiritual heart of the physical body in life. It also lives on as the heart of the spiritual body in the afterlife. The Ab

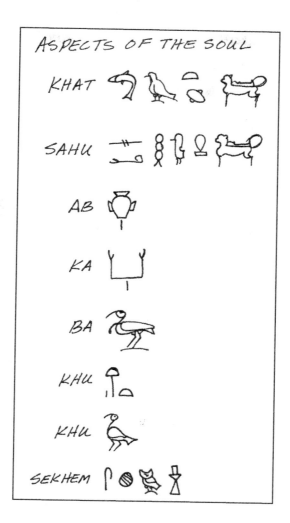

governs the Right and True in a person and their inherent core of ethics. As a power center in the body, the heart was held sacred and unlike the brain was left in the body upon mummification. The ancient Egyptians believed that a person thought with his or her heart, they saw the heart as eternal, with the power to move independently through the planes of consciousness at will, much like an astral umbilical cord.

Ka

The Ka is the mysterious spiritual double, a copy of the physical body on the spiritual plane. Like the astral body it could move at will through the various planes of existence, even returning to the tomb to visit its mummy. Because the Ka was given offerings of food at the tomb, a special door was created in the walls of the tombs or temples called the 'Ka door' through which the Ka could pass freely. The Ka of a person most often dwelt in his or her statue or image. Special instructions were written on the walls of a tomb that specified how to communicate with the Ka.

Ba

The Ba is the spiritual essence of the Ka, and translated means 'sublime or noble'. It dwells inside the Ka and also continues to possess both substance and form after death. Directly linked with the Neters of the heavens, the Ba can revisit the tomb and converse with the deceased and even re-animate them. Like the Ka, the Ba also required food and drink to sustain it, and often partook of the funerary feast.

Khu

As the shining essence of the soul, the Khu can be compared with the Aura or egg of energy that surrounds a person. This essence is eternal and transcends upon death to the realms of the gods. The Khu is a spirit energy that is a part of the collective energy and essence of the Neters/Gods. Upon death, this 'Spiritual intelligence' would be lead by the Neters themselves to dwell in their heavenly abode. In the magical practices, the Khu is regarded as having a direct line of communication with the Gods, much like accessing the super-consciousness during divination.

Sekhem

The Sekhem is likened to the spark or flame, which animates the body, the life-force. An Eternal Flame it represents the fiery will.

Ra himself was referred to as the Sekhem-Ur or Great power, intense, everlasting and possessing of regenerative qualities. The Sekhem flame is the 'Fire of Life' contained in the spine much like the Kundalini Shakti energy of the Hindu tradition.

The raising and manipulating of Sekhem energy are important aspects of Egyptian magical practices and are used in healing rituals, manifestation and even spell-work.

Ren

The Ren is the name of the deceased. It was a magical name given during the initiatory ritual of mummification, a name that only the Gods were privy to. The Ren was also associated with the spoken sound or creation of the name. When written in Hieroglyphs the Ren became a living entity, embodied with a life-force.

Meditation and the Temple

When embarking upon any form of magical practices, one of the most important parts of your work is meditation. Wouldn't it be wonderful if we were all so cosmically in tune that we could flit in and out of ritual with perfect concentration? But alas, most of us residing on this physical plane must teach ourselves to relax and clear our minds of the mundane 'gobble-de-gook' before we can be clear and focused in our intent. Meditation is one of the single most important parts of Egyptian magic, and all magical practices for that matter.

It is also the only way in which we can attune ourselves with our spiritual source (Sekhem), and is part of the discipline aspect of the work. Meditation enables you to build and draw on the power within and experience the different realms of the spiritual and super consciousness.

In ancient times, the priests and priestesses of the temples would fast and perform special temple exercises before meditation much like the Yogis of today. These exercises consisted, in part, of a breathing technique called the 'Sekhem Breath'. The Sekhem was considered the spiritual source and the 'Breath of Life' that animated and nourished the soul.

Evidence of this belief was repeated over and over on temple walls in the form of a God offering an Ankh to the Pharaoh's lips. This symbolized the spark or fire given by Ra as he spoke his sacred vowel of creation. The Sekhem is the 'Fire of Life' that becomes a person's will.

The Egyptians knew that the breath and breathing were keys to the animation of the will. Could they have known that breathing techniques oxygenated the bloodstream and balanced the hormonal glands? I believe so.

The Sekhem Breath is a deep full breath that starts in the diaphragm and then fills the entire chest cavity the same way a full Yoga breath would.

To begin to learn the Sekhem breath, you must first lie flat on the floor. To Practice breathing through your diaphragm begin by placing a book on your stomach. Breathe in deeply. As you breathe, the book should rise with your breath, as you breathe out the book should drop.

EGYPTIAN FIST
POSITION

Once you have mastered that, set the book aside and get ready to do the temple breathing exercises.

Lie flat on the floor with your arms tight against your sides. Make your hands into fists that point thumbs upwards. This is called the Egyptian Fist position, the four fingers representing the four elements and the thumbs, Spirit.

Inhale deeply through your nose, holding your breath for the space of ten seconds. Exhale through your mouth. Then move your right arm straight out to your side. Inhale deeply for ten seconds then exhale through your nose. Repeat this three times then return your right arm to your side. Do the same with your left arm, then bring both arms above your head. Take three deep breaths holding them for ten seconds each. Relax and let your body go completely limp.

When you have completed your breathing exercises and relaxation you are now ready to do your meditation.

There are many and varied methods of meditation and you must find a method that works for you. The method used in Egyptian magic is one that uses concentration, concentration on an object such as a candle flame or an image.

With the candle flame method, start by sitting in an upright position, either cross-legged on the floor or in a straight-backed chair, then place a blue or white candle before you. Stare into the flame of the candle for a couple of minutes until the image of the flame can be seen when you close your eyes. Concentrate on that image while your eyes remain shut. Hold on to it and follow it while breathing fully and normally. As you follow the image of the flame other images from your subconscious will start to appear, these are the first signs that you have entered a meditative state.

The second method of concentration, involves using a statue or object as your 'Flame'. This can be a statue of a deity or an object, such as a pyramid or sphere. Concentrate on that object until everything around it disappears and you will get a sensation of 'going through' the object. Once you have achieved that, you will begin to enter the meditative state as in the candle concentration.

Elements of Purification and Consecration

In the previous chapter, The Working Tools, we had talked about the Purification and Consecration, of yourself, your working tools and your sacred space.

But what about the actual purification and consecration elements themselves?

The oils, incense, and the herbs that are used in all rituals of Egyptian Magic.

In the Inner Sanctum section of this book we will be using many different incense and oils specific to the different rituals of the temples and deities. They are used to 'Perfume' the air to give substance to thought forms and to invite the Gods into our sacred space. Oils and incense were very essential to the magic of the temples, so much so, that special priests and priestesses were trained in the art of Sacred Oil Magic. A healing art that was primarily taught in the temples of Dendera and Edfu. Oils and incense were believed to contain the living essences of plants, plants that were endowed with their own magical properties. A practice, whereby essential oils were used for everything from anointing, healing, mummification and to purify a sacred space. Oil Magic was the very first origins of Aromatherapy.

The Temple Formulary

What follows is a collection of oil and incense recipes used in the temples and various rituals. Some of the recipes are original recipes taken from ancient papyri, while others are my personal recipes from my temple, the Grove of the Green Cobra.

Oils

The first documented method of oil extraction came from ancient Egypt. This is a method that is still used today, and consists of extracting the volatile oils of plants and flowers by means of a carrier oil, such as a light olive oil. In this method, the dried leaves or flowers are placed in a jar of oil. The jar is put in indirect sunlight for a number of days until the oil leaches the essence from the plants to create an essential oil. For the following recipes however, store bought essential oils are more than adequate, and easier to acquire.

Bastet

A sensuous blend to invite the cat goddess Bastet

Lilac	2 parts
Lotus	1 part
Benzoin	½ part
Myrrh	½ part
Sandalwood	3 parts

Egyptian Anointing Oil

Used for all your anointing needs before ritual and in the ritual bath.

Cinnamon	½ part
Myrrh	½ part
Frangipani	1 part
Frankincense	3 parts
Rose	2 parts

Hathor

A very ancient and alluring scent used to invite the goddess Hathor

Rose	3 parts
Neroli	2 parts
Jasmine	2 parts
Vanilla	1 part
Ylang Ylang	1 part

Horus

(For use in rituals that invoke the fiery power of Horus)

Dragons Blood	2 parts
Benzoin	1 part
Sandalwood	2 parts
Balm of Gilead	1 part
Cedar	½ part

Isis
(A recipe with ancient origins, to invite the goddess Isis)

Lotus	2 parts
Rose	3 parts
Civet	½ part
Myrrh	½ part
Vetivert	1 part

Eye of Horus or Wejat Oil
(A scrying oil used to open the third eye and the psychic energies)

Sandalwood	3 parts
Neroli	1 part
Lotus	2 parts
Clove	¼ part
Honeysuckle	2 parts

Egyptian Temple Oil
(Used to invite the presence of the Neters)

Peppermint oil	¼ part
Almond oil	1 part
Lotus oil	2 parts
Myrrh	1 part
Frankincense	3 parts

Osiris
(Used to invite the Lord of the Underworld, Osiris)

Musk	2 parts
Lavender	1 part
Lemon	1 part
Jasmine	½ part
Frankincense	3 parts
Bergamot	1 part
Violet	½ part

Sekhemet

Intense, fiery and healing used to invite the lion-headed goddess
Sekhemet

Dragons Blood	1 part
Jasmine	2 parts
Civet	¼ part
Myrrh	½ part
Sandalwood	3 parts

Tehuti

Used for mental clarity and to invite the god Tehuti

Lavender	2 parts
Frankincense	1 part
Musk	½ part
Lilac	1 part
Narcissus	2 parts

Incense

Used hand in hand with the magical oils, incense is an essential part of Egyptian ceremony and ritual. Like the oils, incense was highly prized and was given to the gods in the form of offerings. The smoke of the incense gave substance to thought forms while the scent invited the various Neters and desired magical properties.

Today, as in ancient times, incense is mainly made from resins combined with herbs and oils. Gum Arabic is then added as a binder and rolled up in fine wood sawdust to form sticks and cones. The Sticks and cones are then dipped in the essential oils and dried. Another easier method, which involves more creativity, is the creation of loose incense. To create the loose incense powder, the fine sawdust is first dyed a desired color using a natural vegetable dye. Once it is dry, the herbs, oils and resins are added to the colored base and mixed thoroughly. The incense can then be ritually 'charged' with the specific purpose for which it was made. To light it you simple pinch the loose incense into a cone shape with your fingers and it is ready to burn.

Bastet

Black base	
Catnip	1 part
Valerian	¼ part
Rose herb and oil	1 part
Black Cat Hair	1 pinch
Orris Root	1 part
Dragons Blood oil	1 part
Frankincense	2 parts
Civet oil	½ part
Heliotrope oil	½ part
Arabian Sandalwood	½ part
Myrrh oil	½ part

Eye of Horus or Wejat Eye

Gold Base	
Balm of Gillead	1 part
Myrrh oil and herb	1 part
Horehound	1 part
Mugwort	2 parts
Clove oil	¼ parts
Frankincense	2 parts

Hathor

Orange Base	
Vanilla oil	½ part
Myrtle herb	1 part
Rose oil and herb	2 parts
Orris Root	2 parts
Ylang Ylang	½ part
Sandalwood oil and herb	1 part

Patchouli oil and herb	1 part
Lotus oil	½ part
Ginseng herb	½ part
Jasmine oil	1 part

Horus

Gold base	
Horehound herb	1part
Copal gum	1 part
Myrrh	½ part
Frankincense	2 parts
Marigold herb	1 part
Neroli	½ part
Ambergris	½ part
Amber oil	½ part
Almond oil	½ part

Kyphi

This powerful incense has been used for thousands of years in the temples to invoke the Egyptian deities. It must be prepared ahead of time on the night of the new moon.

Step 1: Mix your oils, honey, wine and raisins with the dry ingredients: Myrrh resin, juniper berries, Cinnamon, Benzoin resin, Clove, Cassia and Frankincense.

Step 2: Grind into fine powder, then cover and let it sit until the full moon.

Step 3: Place your completed incense under the rays of the full moon and 'Charge' ritually. This is done by first standing before your bowl of incense and placing your hands above the bowl forming a pyramid shape with your thumbs and forefingers. Then take three deep Sekhem breaths. Visualize the energy from the Duat rising up from the ground, into the soles of your feet then up into your heart region. At the same time, bring down the radiant energy of the moon through the crown of your head.

Allow the two energies to conjoin in your Ab (heart) region. Then send that energy down your arms and out through your fingers and into your mixture. As you do say these words:

I Charge thee O'Neter Senfer, (incense) to perfume thy temples, to be as the Au Neheh, to provide for the Neters, to keep pure the Hikau that cometh forth from the mouths of the gods.

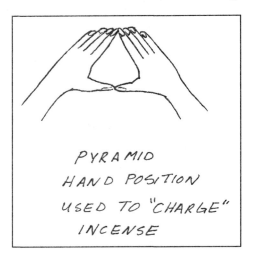

PYRAMID
HAND POSITION
USED TO "CHARGE"
INCENSE

What you will need:

Frankincense	4 parts
Benzoin	2 parts
Gum Arabic resin	2 parts
Myrrh	2 parts
Cedar of Lebannon	1 part
Vetivert	½ part
Cinnamon	½ part
Cardamom	½ part
Clove	½ part
Cassia	½ part

~

Part 2
The Inner Sanctum

~

CHAPTER FOUR

Isis and the Temple of Philae

"I am Isis and I am the Lady of words and power, and I know how to work with words of power, and most mighty are my words."

Isis

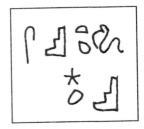

Mistress of Magic and Medicine

What could be more fitting than to begin our journey with Isis and the temple of Philae? Was it not the goddess herself that heralded the rise of the Sothis star and beginning of the Egyptian New Year? The season of Inundation, that brought forth the life giving waters of the Nile.

Isis/Auset, known as the Queen of Heaven, was then and is now the longest worshipped most multi-faceted deity the world has ever conceived. Not only was Isis the first goddess to appear at the dawn of the Egyptian civilization, she was thought to be the first actual Queen of Egypt as well. Her appearance in the Nile Valley coincided with the arrival of the 'Master Race' about 5000B.C.

This was the race of people referred to in W.B. Emery's 'Archaic Egypt', known as the Followers of Horus. The people from the west that had settled in the Nile Valley after the sinking of Atlantis. It was believed at that time, especially by practitioners of the Egyptian religion, that Isis and her husband Osiris were actually real people that became deified through their deeds.

Upon arriving in this new land, Isis and Osiris encountered the primitive peoples that lived along the Nile River. At that time they were wearing the skins of animals, living in mud huts and burying their dead in the fetal position under their homes. In her aspect of a Goddess of Agriculture, Isis taught these people how to plant and harvest corn. In Lower Egypt, in the Land of Ta-Meh, Flax-land, she taught them how to spin and weave the flax into garments. Beer, the national beverage of Egypt, was also attributed to Isis, in her title as the Lady of Bread.

As a Mother Goddess, the very soil of Egypt was attributed to her as 'Isis the Life-Giver'. In this aspect she was attributed to bringing forth the fertile flooding of the Nile. In turn ensuring the fertility of all the living creatures that depended on it.

The story of Isis begins with her birth. She was born the daughter of the Sky Goddess Nut and the Earth God Geb, in the papyrus marshes, in the House of the Green Cobra[1] .While in her Mother's womb, Isis fell in love with her brother Osiris, pledging to him her heart and devotion. Isis and Osiris married and through her example of love and conjugal fidelity, she became the symbol of the ideal wife and mother, a Goddess of the Family. Her love was soon put to the test when her husband was murdered by his evil brother Set, then torn into fourteen pieces and scattered throughout Egypt. Isis, with the help of her sister Nepthys, searched the four corners of the land to find the pieces of his body. They found all the pieces except his phallus, which had been eaten by fish. Isis then fashioned a phallus out of wood and reciting magic spells over her Lord brought him back to life. Osiris was revived for one night, a night of love that produced their son Horus. Isis then took on the aspect of 'the mother of the God', with Horus, the divine son/sun.

Her healing miracle that brought about this holy birth solid-ified her as the Mistress of Magic and Medicine and she is credited as the inventor of many healing drugs. Her healing arts themselves were said to have been taught to her by her uncle Thoth/Tehuti the first High Priest of Egypt. These healing arts took the form of Magical Herbalism, Dream Incubation, (where the patient would be visited in their dreams with a cure from the goddess) and magic spells and rituals. The first medical documents ever written, the medical papyri of ancient Egypt, invoked the power of Isis to aid the patient in healing sickness and to purge the evil of disease from their body.

The Libyan born, Latin writer, Apuleis, summed it up in his ancient text when he invoked Isis as 'The Mother of the Stars, the Parent of Seasons and the Mistress of the whole world'. For as the civilization in the Nile Valley grew and people were able to look beyond their day to day survival, the study of the stars began to fascinate them. Isis herself was associated with the Sothis star, a symbol which can be seen in the hieroglyph of her name. Isis is also depicted with the throne on her head or a large disc with horns. These horns, however, are not the horns of a cow but represent instead, the three phases of the moon. The full, waxing and waning showing her association with the lunar forces.

The very diversity of Isis is what enabled her worship to spread throughout the ancient world. From Egypt to Greece from Greece to Rome where she became among other titles, 'Isis Navigatum, patron goddess of ships and the sea'. Even in the advent of Christianity her worship never died but instead took on another, not so new title, as the Virgin Mary, the mother of God. Though absorbed by other religions, Isian worship never died but was reborn in many ways. Through Gnosticism and the goddess worship by the Knights Templar, through the Golden Dawn and Hermeticism, the revival of Egyptian magic, Wicca and paganism in general.

The mystery of Isis, and her appeal to humankind, has many layers like the veils worn by the High Priestess of the Tarot. Throughout millennium, people, from all walks of life from peasant to Pharaoh, have been able to communicate with her directly. Despite all her lofty attributes she remains, by her very humanness, a goddess for all people and all times.

Magical Attributes:

Name: Isis / Auset

Mistress of Magic and Medicine, Queen of Heaven, Mother of the living Sun, Divine Sorceress, Queen Isis, Isis Myrionymos (the one of the countless names), Isis the Life Giver, The Lady of Great Magic.

Color associations: Deep green, sky blue, black

Planet: Sothis (Sirius), Moon

Metal: Silver

Herbs: Willow, Opium Poppy, Amaranth, Corn, Flax, Lotus

Symbol: The Auset or throne

Stones: Crystal, Amethyst, Ruby, Peridot and Carnelian

Philae and the Temple of Isis
March 2000, 6:30 am

It is early morning as my students and I crowd into the small motorboat that will take us to Philae Island. We have reviewed the ritual the night before and are ready, dressed in pure white garments and adorned in our ceremonial jewelry, our sistrums in hand. We are rocked gently by the current of the Nile, a river that in ancient times symbolized the source of all life. Today, for us, it becomes the source of our spiritual renewal, carrying us to the breast of our Mother Goddess.

There is not much conversation amongst us; many of us are silent in meditation. Presently, as we come around a bend in the river, we see her! A rose red temple dating from Ptolemaic times, Philae Island, the sacred domain of the premiere goddess of Egypt. I am filled with sense of anticipation for it is here our spiritual journey begins…

The Jewel of the Nile:

Known as the 'Jewel of the Nile', Philae and the Temple of Isis is one of the most beautiful and compelling of the ancient temples that have survived up to the present time. This temple, much like the lady herself, has had quite a colorful history. The earliest signs of temple construction go back to the Late Period of Egyptian history and the 25th dynasty during the reign of the Pharaoh Taharqa, approximately 690 to 630 BC.

Philae however, did not rise to its great importance as an Isian center of worship until the Greaco/Roman period. Under Ptolomiac rule, Philae became the premier center for the Cult of Isis. It was here within these sacred walls that the healing miracles of the goddess were performed as well as various festivals and rituals including the 'Birthing of the God' ceremony. In ancient times, there would have been quite the colorful scene year round as royalty and common folk alike made their yearly pilgrimages to the temple of 'The Lady of Great Magic'. Royal barges would have docked at the ancient quay, and a procession would have led them south past the temple of Hathor. They would then head west, opposite the chapel dedicated to the deified architect Imhotep, to the first pylons of the temple. The first pylons, depict even to this day the pharaoh Ptolemy VII dispatching his enemies with the help of the goddess Isis. Beyond these first pylons were sacred areas not open to the general populace in ancient times.

Houses of Eternity

Before we enter further into the temple, I feel it is important to remember the absolute sanctity that was observed in the Egyptian temple at that time. Only then can one appreciate the sense of awe and privilege at being able to walk the halls where only priestesses and pharaohs have trod.

The Egyptian temple was designed to house the 'Neter' or God, and it was specifically built according to esoteric laws. These laws encompassed not only the universal laws of the elements, stars and celestial influences, but also the traditions of each specific deity. For example, it is no

secret that the premier temple to the goddess Isis is located in the life giving waters of the Nile that she herself holds domain over. This and countless other symbolism encompassed in the structure of the temples were carefully planned by the builders of these great monuments. The general layout though, remains constant from temple to temple and is divided by specific areas or temple zones.

These areas, beginning with the very first of the temple approaches or courtyards, increase in sacredness as one enters further into the temple. In ancient times the temple compound would have been walled all the way around. The first area, or large unenclosed courtyard, would have been open to the general populace. Here they could join in the festivals, pay homage and petition the priests and priestesses. The second area beyond the first pylons, the outer court, would be open only to the priests and sometimes a representative of the people. In the third area, the inner halls, only purified priests and priestesses would have been allowed. And finally the inner sanctuary or sanctum could only be visited by Pharaoh or the highest-ranking priests or priestesses. There were many other, outer buildings in the temple complex though, that were open to the public so they could come for healing or the magical advice of a priest or priestess.

Beyond the first pylons

December 1998, 12:00 p.m.

The sun rose high in the brilliant blue sky as our small motorboat docked at the south end of Philae Island. This was the new quay, located opposite one of the oldest monuments of the island. The kiosk of Nectanebo I. Amr, our guide, has timed our visit so that we might avoid the morning tour groups, and have private time in the inner sanctuary for our ritual. With that in mind, I have decided that we should visit the inner temple first and do our sightseeing afterwards.

In a meditative state, we pass through the first pylons into the courtyard of the temple proper. On our left is the mummisia or 'Birth House' dedicated to the pharaoh Ptolemy VI. After our ritual we will visit these sacred rooms and view some of the most beautiful and well- preserved scenes of Isis giving birth to Horus, Isis suckling her infant and the ritual of giving 'the Breath of Life' to the Pharaoh.

As we continue on, we see ahead of us the second pylon entrance. Wide steps guarded by stone lions lead us up to the entrance to the Temple of Isis. The façade of the pylons is graced with magnificent carvings of the goddess on either side, at least fifteen feet in height.

Before entering through the gateway, I must ask everyone to form a line while myself and one of my priestesses perform a sistrum purification on everyone in our group. Amr, is sensitive to the sacredness of this ritual and goes along with it good naturedly. No doubt, Egyptian guides have probably seen it all and more at one time or another!

Having been purified, we are now ready to enter the temple. We are in full awareness of its sacredness, a sacredness that still remains, despite the passage of countless tourists over millennium.

Elaborately carved columns rise far above our heads as we pass through the Main Hall. The doorways decrease in size as we enter further into the temple. They narrow down finally to the doorway of the inner sanctuary. The inner sanctuary, or sanctum, is where we have chosen to perform our ritual of spiritual renewal. It is a small rectangular room perhaps 12' x 12' in size. Her walls are covered with exquisite scenes depicting Isis in her many forms. Isis winged, Isis suckling the infant Horus, Isis with her Lord and husband Osiris, all done in delicate bas-relief. You can almost feel them come alive. The power and energy of the goddess radiates from the walls as we begin our ritual...

Isian Ritual of Renewal

Ritual checklist:

Lotus oil

Frankincense

Salt and water (natron)

Sistrum

Crook and Flail

Ankh

Lotus bowl

Green Beeswax

Chalice

Dates or cakes for libation

Wine or Beer

Incense burner

Dried Scarab beetle

Egyptian working tools, the Sistrum, Ankh, Oil Lamp.

In this, our first Egyptian ritual, we will be calling upon the powers of Isis and the Scarab God Khepera to lead us into a spiritual renewal. This is a ritual designed for group magic, and as such the participants will want to form an informal circle to discuss what areas of their life they wish to bring renewal to. This is done not to spy on each other's desires, but so that in true working group spirit, each person has the same vision of each other's goal to work with. When this is done, each person shall inscribe their will individually on small one-inch squares of parchment or papyrus.

Ritual

Before commencing the ritual, the temple area must be consecrated with natron water and frankincense. The High Priestess (Yours Truly) leads the participants in a serpentine procession to the temple. At the entrance to the temple, the Sistrum Purification is performed on all who might enter the sacred space. When this is done the participants enter the temple from the east and take their places. At this time a healing meditation is led by the High Priestess. In this meditation the Egyptian flame is brought up into each and every one present. (The temple dancer begins to raise the energy through music and dance) After the meditation and grounding, the participants in the place of their respective goddesses do their invocations to the four directions starting from the east and the land of the rosy dawn.

East, Nieth: "Hail thou that ruleth the east, Lord Duamutef, jackal headed son of Horus, Nieth warrior goddess and protectress come forth from the abyss to lend your presence here."

West, Selkit: "Hail thou that ruleth the south, Lord Quesennuf, falcon headed son of Horus, Selkit scorpion goddess of magic come forth O' soul of the ram of the west."

North, Nephtys: "Hail to thou that ruleth the north, Lord Hapi, ape headed son of Horus,Nephtys, goddess of the underworld come forth from the lands of rebirth at the mouth of the Nile."

South, Sekhemet: "Hail to thou that ruleth the south, Lord Imsety, human headed son of Horus, Sekhemet lioness of the desert who guards the eternal flame come forth from the red land of the Ureaus."

After the four sons of Horus and the Neters or Gods of the four directions have been called in, the High Priestess shakes her sistrum five times to invoke Isis.

High Priestess:

"Hika!

Hika!

Hika!

Hika!

Hika!"

"Isis per aha! I invoke thee O' mistress of magic and medicine, who cometh forth from the Papyrus marshes, from the House of the Green Cobra. Just as Osiris heard your cry, we beseech you to be here now, as we do honor to this time of spiritual fertility and renewal. A UA PEST EM AaH PERT!"

After the invocation, Sekhmet in place of fire comes forth to light the oil lamp. One by one the members light their wills from the flame and drop them into a small thurible. When they have all burned to ashes the High priestess adds nine drops of lotus oil and the powdered scarab to the mixture forming a paste.

The green beeswax is then placed in the hands of the member who would be Osiris. The High Priestess takes up the Ankh from the altar and places it against Osiris' lips. Saying these words: "Awake! Awake! Osiris! From your realms of the underworld. Awake! Awake! My love so that the world shall be reborn from the darkness, and with this awakening the rebirth of our desires on all levels."

The High Priestess then places the paste mixture in the center of the green sheet of beeswax. Osiris forms it into an egg shape. He then passes it among the participants so they can lend their hand to the shaping of the egg. When the 'egg' is complete Osiris places it on the altar and proceeds to roll it east to west three times. All the members focus on their desires at this time.

Osiris then invokes the scarab god Khepera:

"Khepera, per aha! Lend thy strength to this your cosmic egg, formed from magic and the secret effluvium of our desires."

"ANET HRA K AMUN RA!"

The High Priestess holds her sistrum aloft:

"Lady Isis, Daughter of the Sun, it is from you we receive the blessings of renewal, go forth now to the seed ground of the stars from which you came, may you burn like Uta the eternal flame in our hearts forever."

Starting in the east the Neters are dismissed:

"Return, return O' lord of the east, Duamutef, jackal headed son of Horus, Neith warrior goddess sheath thine arrows in the land of the Abyss."

"Return, return O' lord of the west, Quebsennuf, falcon headed son of Horus, Selkit goddess of magic return to the land of your birth."

"Return, return O' lord of the north, Hapi, ape headed son of Horus, Nephtys goddess of the underworld return to your watery realm."

"Return, return O' lord of the south, Lord Imsety, human headed son of Horus, Sekhemet lioness of the desert return to your vigil of the eternal flame."

When the ritual is over a libation is shared. It can be a traditional one of beer and honey cakes or dates.

The symbolism of this ritual comes from the Sacred Scarab Beetle. The scarab beetle acquired magical significance from the ancient Egyptians because of the curious way it would roll its dung balls containing its eggs, from east to west. Those directions that related to birth and regeneration. These actions lent spiritual significance to the scarab beetle, which in turn deified it into the god Khepera the Scarab Headed God of renewal, regeneration and fertility.

Temple of Isis at Philae
March 15 2000

Our arrival at Philae this morning, had been carefully planned to avoid the hordes of tourists at this time of the year. It soon became apparent though that we had not planned carefully enough. No sooner had we reached the inner sanctuary, when another large group landed at the dock.

We decided then, that we would only have private time to do our meditation inside the Sanctuary. The ritual itself, would have to be done elsewhere in the temple complex. With that in mind, we gathered around the altar and I led us in a meditation to align ourselves with the Isian energy.

From there we proceeded outside to the temple of Hathor, an exquisite temple dedicated to Philae by Cleopatra VII, that stands facing east, overlooking the Nile. The day was beautiful, the sky and waters shone a brilliant blue, a fine setting for our dedication to Isis...

Dedication to Isis
This ritual is to be performed as a dedication of oneself to the goddess Isis. In contemplating that dedication, the participants have meditated beforehand on what their sacrifice would be in the service of the Mother. The sacrifices are not the blood sacrifices, that were sometimes done in ancient times, but rather personal sacrifices to petition the help of the goddess with a particular goal. For example: To gain success over a health matter you might burn a candle in honor of Isis every night for a moon cycle or plant a herb in her name to secure a new job opportunity. The specific sacrifice to be done is usually given to a person in a dream or a meditation, much like the Dream Incubation that was practiced in the temples in ancient times.

Ritual Checklist
1" x 1" pieces of papyrus of parchment
Isian incense
Salt and water (natron)
Ankh
Sistrum
Beer and libation cakes
Statue of the goddess

We begin this ritual, as with all temple works, with the purification of the temple area and the participants. When that is done, the four sons of Horus and the Neters are invoked as in the previous ritual. The High Priestess then leads the group in meditation to align them with the Isian energy. The temple dancer begins to raise the energy through music and dance. Raising her hands in the KA position the High Priestess invokes Isis:

High Priestess: "Isis per aha, I invoke thee, O' Divine Mother and Mistress of Charms and Enchantments, You who maketh Osiris whole in the underworld, Who knoweth the secret name of Ra, Who healed Horus by the use of talismans and words of power, come forth now to receive these sacrifices, so that your people can uphold your place in Heaven."

The High priestess then shakes her sistrum five times saying:

"Hika!
Hika!
Hika!
Hika!
Hika!"

One-by-one the participants are anointed with oil on their forehead and lips. The High Priestess then draws the Sekhem power up through her Ankh and places it to the lips of each person in turn. This symbolizes the opening of the mouth ritual.

Each person repeats after the priestess:

"By words and deeds I dedicate myself to Isis."

The sacrifices are then placed in the thurible to burn, the Neters are dismissed, and the libation shared. The ashes of our wills are then taken to the west side of the temple complex, near the nilometer, and are cast in the waters of the Nile.

This next ritual is one of our Temple Rituals. It is intended to show the meaning behind the teachings of the goddess by way of the Sacred Symbols. I have not as yet, had the opportunity to perform this ritual in the temples. So many rituals, so little time, so maybe next trip!

The Sacred Symbols of Isis

Ritual checklist:

    1 blue veil
    1 red feather
    Water vessel
    Star
    Lion symbol
    2 keys

As usual the ritual is begun with the purification of the temple area. It is purified with frankincense and natron water at the four quarters. A silent consecration is then performed by the High Priestess and Priest in the roles of Isis and Osiris.

A pause is then taken for meditation. A Member in the role of Anubis, takes his place as guardian of the Eastern portal. Isis and Osiris are seated in the west. Isis invokes her Sekhem power while the rest of the members wait beyond the east portal.

Osiris: "I am Osiris-Amenti, lord of the Abyss who is seated here at the threshold of transformation. Seated to my left, is my wife and Queen Isis, who hath maketh me whole in the Underworld. Who possesseth the Sacred Symbols to unlock the fire of Sekhem in our breasts and who hath integrated all matter of great wisdom in man. Isis Per Aha, unfold to me O' Queen the symbols of Divine Wisdom."

Isis: "Osiris per Aha! My lord and husband. To see beyond the veil of Amentet, the earthly plane, you must first look to the East, the land of Seket-Hetep, the rosy dawn."

Anubis: "O' lord there is a lady that waits at the portal."

Osiris: "Bid her come forth."

Maat comes forth carrying the red feather.

Osiris: "Lady what symbol do you hold?"

Maat: "This feather is the symbol of Truth. Truth and knowledge create courage, courage of the wise, so that they may have no fear in the face of both suffering and joy. So that they may grow in harmony with the rhythm of the cosmos. So they may discover the justice of The Great Law in all things from life to death to life."

Maat places the feather at the feet of Isis and takes her place next to the goddess.

Anubis: "There is another who waits at the portal."

Osiris: "Bid her come forth."

Sekhemet enters carrying a lion symbol.

Osiris: "Lady what symbol is your diadem?"

Sekhemet: "Osiris-Amenti, I am Sekhemet, daughter of Fire, the Sekhem force within. I drink the blood of the enemies of Truth.

My symbol is Courage and Magical strength. Fire is the element of love, to truly love one must not fear and in not fearing you may attain courage of the heart. This is your magical strength, your truth that is Faith."

(Sekemet places the symbol at the feet of Isis)

Anubis: "There is another who stands at the portal."

Osiris: "Bid her enter."

Nepthys enters carrying a vessel of water.

Osiris: "Lady what symbol do you reveal?"

Nepthys: "This water is a symbol of the Lifestream, our journey from birth to death to birth in the land of Tem, a land where the spirits of these worlds have much to teach us. Where our Ba soul passes from the physical body to spirit and on again in a never ending cycle."

Nepthys places her vessel at the feet of Isis.

Anubis: "There is one more who stands at the portal."

Osiris: "Bid her enter."

Nut enters carrying the symbol of the star.

Osiris: "Lady what truths do you impart to us?"

Nut: "The symbol of the Stars. The stars hold the fate of humankind. Their existence is written in the starry night. Each person is attuned to the rhythm and sound of the celestial bodies, and only by following the rules of the Gods will they attain harmony."

Nut places her symbol at the feet of Isis.

Osiris to Isis: "My beloved, is there more you would reveal?"

Isis: (Lifting her veil) "These symbols together bring MAA NA AUSAR, a spiritual alignment of the worlds that recognize Truth, Courage, Rebirth, Fate and magical power. And through these keys before your death you will be able to enter the realm of Torture and the realm of Eternal Joy, you will see the great law of sowing and harvesting. For all that we do is sowing and all of our experiences and adventures are our harvests. All these things go forth to the seed ground of the stars, to eventually reach perfection, so we may never return to the earthly plane but live forever in the land of Eternal Joy."

Osiris: "It is only right that you should be seated beside me in the west, the land of transformation for your keys shall unlock the hidden knowledge of the invisible world. So that we may communicate with higher beings so that we may participate in the evolution of the universe, always remembering the guiding principles of Knowledge, Will, Courage and Silence."

At the closing of the ritual the Libation is shared. The Symbols remain on the altar, so that the participants can meditate on their meaning.

Divination of the Lamp

On my last tour to Egypt in 2000, I made a fabulous discovery while exploring deep into the Khan El Khalili bazaar. This bazaar, the oldest surviving bazaar in the world, consists of hundreds of little shops placed side by side and on top of each other in colorful disarray. That day I had decided to visit a brass shop that Linda, one of my fellow travelers had visited before on her last trip to Egypt.

After much searching and many dead ends we located the shop, located at the top of some ancient, winding, stone steps. Steps so worn from time and the passage of human feet that the middle of the step was just one big groove. Once at the top, we entered a small shop piled full of brass trinkets and curios. They winked at us from every available surface, every shelf and even hung from the ceiling. Linda went straight away to give the owner of the shop her order. I hung back and started poking around in the curious array of objects. Then I saw it! Covered in dust, tucked away among some tarnished chains and pots. The perfect oil lamp! I was irresistibly drawn to it. When I lifted it out of that incongruous pile, I could feel the energy sing through it. This was a lamp that had been used for divination before! I was hardly able to keep the gleam of anticipation from my eyes as I asked the proprietor what he would take for it. Knowing full well that this was to be an important working tool, I shocked myself by making only a token attempt at bargaining.

The method of Oil lamp Divination

Oil Lamp Divination, or Vessel Inquiry, as it was referred to by the ancient Egyptians, is still practiced today by followers of the Egyptian Tradition. In ancient times, an elaborate ritual was performed to invoke the Spirit of the Lamp, The spirit itself being a kind of deity that presided over all oil lamps much like the proverbial 'Genie of the Lamp'. Once this spirit was invoked it would convey its message through the petitioner or in the case where a priest would be performing the ritual, it would sometimes be channeled through a young boy.

The oil lamp would reveal its messages through the use of the element fire. Much like scrying into a cauldron or a candle flame. The fire would animate the life force or Sekhem energy of the spirit coaxing it to reveal its secrets. The Oil Lamp was such an important divination tool that whole papyrus texts were devoted to the rituals and spells of it use. Special wicks for the Lamp were prepared ahead of time using a linen strip in which magical spells and invocations had been inscribed. The lamp would be filled with Oasis oil, a very fine olive oil, and sometimes that oil would be scented with a magical essence, such as Myrrh, Rose, Neroli or the mystical but now extinct Blue Lotus. Today modern practitioners have had to make do with inscribing on ready made wicks and adding the sacred oils to store bought lamp oil.

The divination ritual itself is best done when the moon is high and full in the sky. For this you must prepare for the ritual by first applying green eye paint to your eyes, taking care to outline them in black. Set out an offering of bread, fruit and wine. Insert your wick that has been inscribed ahead of time into the lamp. Raise your hands in the KA position to invoke the Spirit of the Lamp as you do so, speak these words:

"Speak to me Hamset, God of the Gods of Darkness, every demon, every shade that is in the West and East, He that hath died, rise up to me! O', thou living soul, O' thou breathing soul, may my vessel go forth here today for the sake of Isis the Great!

Menash, Menanf! (Repeat 5 times)

Open Tat! Open Nap! (Open my eyes, open thine eyes!)"

After speaking the invocation gaze into the flame of the Lamp, the flame will dance and twirl as it reveals its messages. When you are done thank the Spirit of the Lamp and ask it to return to its own realm in peace and bringing harm to none that cross its path.

Egyptian Spellwork

Spellwork and magic were part of the everyday life of the ancient Egyptians. In the magical society in which they lived, they communicated and petitioned their gods for a myriad of purposes both personal and spiritual. Spells and enchantments were ways to gain control over situations and to seek divine intervention. In the following chapters I will be sharing with you some of the spells from the Isian tradition.

Lotus Protection Spell

This magic spell makes use of a special talisman that you create to protect the home from all forms of negativity that might try to enter.

What you will need:

1 piece of papyrus or parchment 5" x 5"

Black ink

Orris Root Powder

Lotus Oil

On a Friday night when the moon is full draw your best rendition of a lotus flower on the front of the piece of papyrus. If you can't find some plain papyrus you can use a piece of parchment paper of a light color such as off –white or gold. On the back of the paper draw these three Hieroglyphs:

Isis/Auset   strengtheneth   thy habitation

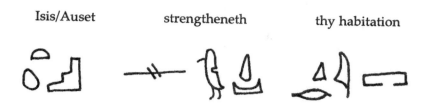

When you are finished, anoint the paper with the lotus oil, then sprinkle Orris root powder over it on both sides. As you do so, say these words: "Spiral of gold and wings unfold, Isis bless and protect me."

Leave the talisman overnight in the moonlight. The next day place it over your front doorway to lend protection from all that may enter.

Aloe Love Spell

To weave a spell of true love, these ancient words of enchantment shall fly past the barriers of time to make you irresistible to the object of your desire.

What you will need:

    3 pieces of papyrus or parchment
    Black ink
    Dried or powdered Aloe
    2 smooth river stones
    Red wine or juice

On a night three days before the full moon, write on the papyrus pieces the name of your intended lover. On the reverse side inscribe the hieroglyph of the heart or AB.

The first night burn one of the papers in the ceramic dish, visualizing the face of your lover in the flame. Let it burn completely to ashes. Repeat these steps for the following nights, remembering to do your visualization. On the third night, after you have burnt the last piece of papyrus. Grind the aloe between the two stones, grind it into a fine powder and mix it in with the ashes. Stir the mixture nine times with the second finger of your left hand, the finger of the heart. As you do say these words:

"Mighty Isis, let the heart of _____ be turned to me,

Let it be turned in joy, let it be turned in love,

for as long as the gods may grant it."

When you are done, put the powder into the wine or juice. Serve it to your lover when he or she comes to call. You will become irresistible!

The Amulet of the Buckle

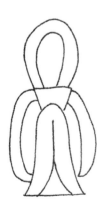

An Amulet is a magically charged object that is created for a specific purpose. Amulets were used profusely in ancient Egypt. They were used for anything from love and protection to being sewn into the wrappings of the mummy to prepare the deceased in the Afterlife. The Amulet of the Buckle represents a buckle or knot that was said to be the sign of grief that Isis made upon learning of the murder of her husband Osiris. At which time she cried out 'SAK-ER-ME' (come to me) to the universe.

Traditionally the amulet is red in color, the color of the 'Blood of the Goddess', and in ancient times was made from Carnelian, Red Jasper or the wood of the Sycamore tree. The use of this amulet was to protect the wearer from sickness and negative influences. These days a very comparable amulet can be made from self-hardening clay or carved in wood.

The creation of your amulet should take place on a Friday night in the first quarter of the moon. Begin by fashioning it out of your red 'Fimo' clay. When you are done put it in the oven for the prescribed time. When it is done remove it from the oven and let it cool completely. It should turn out red in color like the holy blood of Isis. Next wrap it carefully in the white cloth and place it on your altar. On the night of the full moon uncover your amulet, and hold it up to the lunar light. Anoint it with a little oil of Neroli, as you do so, say these words:

"The blood of Isis and the strength of Isis, and the words of power of Isis shall be mighty to act as powers to protect this great and divine being, and to guard him/her from him that would do unto him/her anything that he holdeth in abomination."

After creating your amulet and charging it with these words of power it is ready to be worn or carried on your person.

Isis Bless!

The Sacred Dreaming True

Dream Incubation, or the seeking of prophetic dreams was a large part of the spiritual and magical practices in ancient Egypt. Each temple had an area specially designated for people to enter and receive prophetic dreams. These areas were called the Sanitoria, and were used as healing rooms as well. In ancient times it was a common practice for anyone who needed spiritual guidance in his or her lives to spend the night in the temple. Specially trained priests and priestesses that specialized in Dream Interpretation; The Scribes of the House of Life were available to the populace for consultation.

Dream interpretation and healing dreams were used before treating a patient for an illness or before surgery. Through dreams the Neters or Gods could be communicated with. Dream incubation in the 'House of the God' would ensure contact with that specific deity. The Dreaming True ritual is a ritual in which you will attempt to contact the goddess Isis through your dreams. Don't get discouraged if this does not happen the first night, sometimes, it may take up to two weeks.

What you will need:

A statue or picture of Isis
An orange beeswax candle
Lotus oil

Begin your ritual when the moon is high in the sky about 9:00 pm. Take three deep 'Sekhem' breaths in through the mouth and out through the nose. Relax and meditate on the goddess. Place the orange candle in front of her and light it. Anoint yourself on the forehead with a little of the lotus oil. As you do so, recite these words:

"Lady of Great Magic, I beseech thee this night to send unto me a sacred dream, so I may be as the seer in your great shrine, so I may receive the great truths that you may give me, so I may go forth by day with the blessings of your great knowledge."

When you are finished go to sleep, the blessings of the goddess are sure to follow!

CHAPTER FIVE

Osiris and the Temple of Abydos

"Lord of the heavens and of the earth, of the underworld and of the waters, of the mountains, and all which the sun goeth around his course."

The Lord of Eternity

As legend would have it, a great cry was heard when the firstborn son of Nut the sky goddess was born, proclaiming him the 'Lord of all the Earth'. His name was Osiris and he emerged from the womb already crowned as the first king of Egypt.

One of the oldest gods in ancient Egypt, Osiris was said to have come from the land of the west, Amenti, along with his wife and consort Isis. His appearance in the Nile valley can be documented as early as the first dynasty, approximately 4000 B.C. where images of Osiris are depicted on a mace head of the Pharaoh Narmer, and depicted again as well on a wooden plaque of Hesepti the fifth king of the first dynasty.

Osiris whom the Egyptians called Ozer, became the first example of the Priest King, a benevolent peaceful ruler that brought civilization to a land where chaos and even cannibalism existed. Osiris was credited with introducing the first religious system, a written language and the knowledge of planting and harvesting. He went on to establish the first unified capital of Egypt, Abydos, which became the center of the Cult of Osiris.

During the twenty-eight years of his reign there was peace and prosperity in the land of Egypt. On that twenty-eighth year however a storm cloud was brewing, a cloud in the form of Set the God of Chaos, the covetous brother of Osiris who was said to have had a forced birth into the world through an open wound. Set envied his handsome brother and coveted the throne. He formed an evil plan with the help of Queen Aso of Ethiopia along with seventy-two co-conspirators, a plan that would do away with his brother Osiris.

Set waited until Isis was away to put his plan into motion. He bribed one of Osiris' servants to gain the king's exact measurements. He then had a beautiful chest created of a dark wood inlaid with silver and precious stones.

When the chest was completed he held a grand banquet. At the banquet he invited all the guests to try and fit in to the chest.

He promised that whomever could fit into it could have it. Naturally, none of the guests could fit into it. Osiris was then invited to try. He lay down in the chest to find it was a perfect fit!

Set and his conspirators rushed to nail the chest closed. After it was nailed shut they poured molten lead over it to seal it. Osiris trapped and entombed within the beautiful chest was taken down to the banks of the Nile. The chest that was his coffin was tossed into the river.

He floated for miles before the chest finally washed to shore on the island of Byblos. Buffeted by the waves, it came to rest on the shore and became entangled in the roots of a Tamarisk tree. The tree, nourished by the energy of Osiris, grew overnight to gigantic proportions. The King of Byblos, Melcarthus, was amazed when he saw the size and beauty of the tree. He ordered it to be cut down and made into a pillar to support the roof of his palace, never guessing that within this pillar was the chest that contained the body of the king of Egypt, Osiris.

When Isis returned from her travels she discovered the

betrayal of Set and the death of her lord. Grief stricken, she set out in search for the chest that contained Osiris. She communed with the spirits and from them learned that the chest had come to rest in Byblos.

Disguising herself as a humble hairdresser she traveled to Byblos. At the well in the center of town she saw the queen of Byblos and her handmaidens. She approached them and breathed sweet perfume upon their hair and clothes. The queen, Astarte, was charmed and awarded the beautiful stranger the care of her son.

That night Isis came back to the great hall where the pillar stood. She added wood to the fire and thrust the young prince into the flame. When the queen arrived she saw her son twisting in the flames and screamed out for his life. Quickly, Isis retrieved him from the fire. She admonished the queen telling her that her interruption had deprived her son of immortality. She then revealed her identity and told queen Astarte her story. The queen having compassion for Isis' plight gave her the pillar as a parting gift.

Isis retrieved the chest and hid it in the papyrus marshes of Buto, but soon it became true that she did not hide it well enough.

Set hunting by the rays of the moon discovered the chest and removed the body of Osiris. He tore it to pieces and scattered it throughout the land of Egypt. Discovering Set's deed, Isis and her sister Nepthys frantically searched the land. They retrieved all of the scattered pieces with the exception of Osiris' phallus, which had been eaten by fish. Isis fashioned a new one from wood and together with her sister and the help of Anubis the jackal-headed funerary god, they performed the first embalming rite. Osiris was made whole again. Isis spoke words of magic over her lord and his vitality was restored, Isis and Osiris had one night of love in which Isis conceived their son Horus. Osiris then went on to rule the underworld becoming the first archetype for the mummy to be known as the Lord of the Underworld, a Lord of Rebirth that ruled by night.

Just as Ra ruled by the rays of the sun, Osiris ruled by the cycles of the moon.

His powers took on many associations, chiefly agricultural, because plants and animals were thought to propagate under the humid influence of the lunar rays.

As a god of regeneration, he was often depicted as a spirit of the corn. Carvings from the walls of Philae show him lying supine with ears of corn sprouting from his body, while water is poured upon him by temple priests. Its inscription reads:

"This is the form of Him whom one may not name, Osiris of the mysteries who springs forth from the returning waters."

This curious symbolism can not help but to draw on parallels with other 'Sacrificial Lords' whose bodies, when scattered upon the land, promoted new crops. Even Isis herself, collected his scattered body parts in a corn sieve.

Osiris also had strong associations with trees, and his symbol the Djed pillar, was none other than a stylized version of the Tamarisk pillar that became his sarcophagus. In his 'Green Man' aspect he was seen as a green-faced mummy, wearing the white crown of the south, the inundation of the Nile was naturally associated with Osiris as well.

Festivals held in his honor had people ritually planting corn in the new fertile soil. His powers of regeneration did not only extend to the land and animals but to the regeneration and rebirth of the soul as well. From his kingdom in the land of Amenti, he presided over the judgment of the dead whose souls had made their journey into the Duat or underworld. Later in Egyptian history he became associated with the sacred Apis bulls of the Serapeum. Sacrificial bulls were embalmed and magnificently entombed so that their souls would join with Osiris, to be reborn as the fulfillment of the desires and wishes of the populace.

Magical Attributes:

Name: Osiris, Ozer, Au-Sar,

Symbol: Throne with the eye above it, the mummy, Djed Pillar, Bull and Pine Cone

Color: Green

Metal: Pale Gold

Number: 1

Tools: The Crook and Flail

Herbs: Dittany of Crete

Key Words: Sovereignty, Stability, and Rebirth

Journey to Abydos

March 18th 2000, 6:00 am

This morning we are in need of an early start if we are to make the journey to the Temple of Osiris at Abydos. Our plans to visit this temple have been hastily arranged, as we did not know until we landed in Cairo if we would be able to visit Abydos. It is a long and arduous bus ride through the countryside but we have complete faith in our guide Amr, to get us there safely.

Though it is early in the morning I can feel tendrils of excitement rise up my spine at the prospect of Abydos. It has been quite a while since I have seen it. In ancient times, pilgrims made the journey to Abydos at least once in their lifetime to pay homage to the God of rebirth.

Today even at this early hour we are traveling prepared to do ritual, dressed in our white
robes and packing with us all the necessary working tools.

We drive through miles and miles of farmland where Egyptian farmers, the Fellaheen, toiled in the fields where their small barefoot children played in the yards of mud brick homes, at ease crawling over the backs of huge water buffalo. During our journey we are privileged to see a rare sight. A traditional tribal wedding called a Zeffa, which revealed the bride riding in a curtained seat on the back of a camel. Musicians and well-wishers heralded their progress through a recently plowed field.

Finally through many miles and several checkpoints, we get to Abydos. The small town itself is a collection of ancient mud-brick dwellings and narrow streets reminiscent of a time nearly 2000 years before. Our bus stops at the entrance of the temple and we file out.

The Seat of the God

Abydos, one of the oldest and best preserved temples from ancient times has a long and mystical history. The original temple dates back to the first dynasties of the Old Kingdom. It is also the seat of one of the oldest cities in the ancient world, Tinis. Here, pilgrims would travel each year to pay homage to the Lord of the Underworld Osiris, a goal that every Egyptian hoped to accomplish at least once in his or her lifetime.

The annual festival of Osiris was held in the spring. During this festival the temple priests would carry the statue of the god from his sanctuary to his burial mound called Umm el Quaab, the 'Mother of pots', where the pilgrims would lay their offerings in clay pots. Thousands upon thousands of their pottery shards litter the area around the temple even to this day.

Abydos was also an important religious center in ancient times. Known as the City of the Dead, where the most important relic in Egypt, the head of Osiris, was said to be preserved. Many Pharaohs built their shrines and placed their cenotaphs, here, in hopes of communing with the God in his underworld paradise.

On the surface this temple appeared to serve the dead in death; however, its real purpose was to serve them in life,- the Afterlife.

This temple that housed the God of the Dead was a recreation of the underworld in which he dwelled. For beneath the hallowed halls of the shrine was a mysterious font of immortality. The Osirion, is an underground well with many conduits symbolizing the rivers of the underworld. A small stone sarcophagus and a canopic chest which at one time held the internal organs stands on the island in the middle of the underground well. The waters themselves represent the primordial waters of Nu, the waters of creation, the fluid of transformation and rebirth.

Inside the temple are seven individual sanctuaries built in the time of Sethos I. Each long, rectangular, room is dedicated to a specific God or Goddess. The exquisite carvings and artwork on the walls are pure, still containing their original colors undiluted by Greek or Roman influence.

Once inside, the temple we walk through is a labyrinth of hallways empty but for a few scattered Egyptologists. We stop at the entrance to the sanctuary of Isis, the perfect place for our ritual to Osiris.

Inside the sanctuary, beautiful life-like carvings line the walls, their original colors still vibrant after thousands of years. The pictures tell the story of the death and resurrection of Osiris, depicted on his funeral couch with Isis and Nepthys at his head and feet chanting the magic spells that will make him whole again. One of the most compelling of them is a depiction of Osiris in an almost ecstatic state with a hawk hovering over his restored phallus.

Due to the protective attitude shown to us by the guards, we have decided to do a simple ritual of rebirth and renewal, one that will infuse the regenerative energy of Osiris in to the hopes and wishes of each of our lives.

Osirian Rite of Rebirth

As a god of rebirth and regeneration Osiris was born again through the magic of Isis' love. In this Osirian rite each one of us shall celebrate a renewal in our lives on all levels.

Ritual checklist

White Altar Cloth
Frankincense
Beer

Bread
Small Sarcophagus
Parchment papers (petitions)
Lotus oil

The first step in our ritual is to prepare a small altar. There is no stone altar in the Sanctuary, so I decide to place a white cloth in the center of the floor to serve as a makeshift altar. The Ankh, incense burner, bread, and beer and a small sarcophagus are placed on the altar. The incense is lit and the Four Corners are censed starting with the east, west, north and south.

Priestess: "I have come unto thee, O' Osiris Khenti-Amentet to purify this temple so it may serve thee in a state of cleanliness."

Once the sanctuary is cleansed another participant anoints each person on the forehead with the Lotus oil. Everyone joins hands in meditation. We begin by taking some deep Egyptian breaths, to stimulate the Sekhem energy in our bodies. As we breath deeply and fully we can feel the stone floor beneath our feet vibrating. The whole temple itself acting like a huge power conduit. I ask everyone to visualize themselves standing on the petals of a giant blue lotus, whose roots go deep into the water. The energy courses up and down our spines as though we had been touched by a large tuning fork.

High Priestess: "Osiris Per Aha, I invoke thee, King of the Underworld, that resides in the House of Eternity. Come forth this day to grant us our desires. Just as Isis gave you the gift of life so shall it be restored to us this day."

The small sarcophagus is taken up by a priestess, which she in turn presents to each person.

Priestess: "Place in this vessel the wills of your desires."

Each person places a small folded parchment into the sarcophagus. Previously, each person has meditated on those things in their lives that they wished to bring renewal and rebirth to. When everyone has placed his or her petition into the sarcophagus it is returned to the altar. I then take the Ankh and pass it through the incense smoke.

High Priestess: "May this sacred perfume purify this tool so that it may serve to bring forth the 'Breath of Life'."

The purified Ankh is then held up and placed upon each person's lips.

High Priestess: "Receive the Breath of Life, A Ua Pest EM Aaa PERT!"

After each person has received the 'Breath of Life', we return to the meditation, we begin to ground the energies that we have raised.

High Priestess: "We are purified in the land of Amenti, our Lord Osiris has been reborn in our hearts. We receive from this temple what we need to nourish the Khat and the KA, we release that which we no longer need into the primordial waters of Nu beneath our feet."

High Priestess: "We pay homage to our Lord Osiris, may you return whole to the realm of Amenti, may your bread never decay and your beer never go stale."

The ritual is concluded with a libation of beer and bread, some of which is saved to nourish the BA. After we leave the temple, we bring our little sarcophagus to the sandy dunes where the pottery shards of ancient pilgrims litter the sand. With our hands we bury the petitions.

Raising the Djed Pillar

From the story of Osiris, we now know a little about the symbolism behind the Djed pillar. In the myth, it represented the Tamarisk tree that enveloped the chest containing the body of the God. The KA of Osiris, that shining light of the soul, was so vibrant that it nourished the tree, causing it to grow to majestic proportions. Coveted by the King of Byblos, it was cut down to serve as a pillar to support the roof of his palace. Already this pillar had taken on new symbolic meaning. First as the sacred tree that housed the Tree- Spirit of Osiris, a concept that would have many ritual associations. The Greek philosopher Plutarch details some of these rituals in which a pine tree would be cut down and hollowed out. The wood from the center of the tree would be fashioned into a likeness of Osiris. He would then be placed or 'buried' back into the hollow tree.

In this aspect the Djed takes on the characteristics of fertility and growth, a phallic symbol, much like the maypole, whose energies propagate the life-stream.

Another association comes from the Djed as a pillar, a pillar to hold up the roof of a palace. The palace is likened to the body or vessel and the pillar becomes a symbol of support and stability.

Magically, the Djed is a very interesting concept: The shape is Phallic, representing fertility and virility, the color is green for growth and renewal and the four cross-bars at the top represent the four elements of creation: Air, Fire, Water and Earth. The Djed Pillar is truly the quintessential representation of creation.

In the following ritual we will raise the Djed pillar inside of us, bringing the energies of rebirth and stability into our physical, emotional and spiritual bodies.

Ritual Checklist:

    Sandalwood oil
    Natron water
    Straight backed chair (Symbolic throne/seat
       of Osiris)
    Osiris incense
    Ritual time: Full Moon

To begin this ritual you must first start by purifying your body in a Natron bath.

To do this, you add ½ cup of sea salt and one tablespoon of bicarbonate of soda to your bath water. Relax in your bath and allow all negative thoughts and energies to leave your body.

When you are done, towel off then anoint yourself with the sandalwood oil. Anoint all the chakra points starting with the crown. Then put on a comfortable, loose robe, preferably a ritual robe. Light the incense. With your hands, fan some of the smoke over your body. When you are finished take a seat in the straight backed chair. Place your hands in your lap in the Egyptian Fist position. Begin by taking five deep Sekhem breaths, in through the mouth and out through the nose holding each breath for a count of nine. With your legs uncrossed and your feet flat on the ground begin to visualize your feet as the roots of a tree going down deep into the earth. Imagine that tree becoming one with your spine, supporting it and strengthening it. Feel your roots going deep into the earth into the underworld where they connect to the golden orb at the center of the earth, the birthplace of the moon. Draw that energy up into your body. Through the soles of your feet, up into your legs, your torso, your chest and AB center up through your neck then out the top of your head. Visualize the energy slowly flowing back down over you like a fountain. As you do, visualize its fluid like the colors of the elements. First yellow then red, blue then finally black. As you bathe in the light of creation, contemplate each elemental property. Infuse the elemental energy into your body. When you are done bring it back through the top of your head and slowly back down your spine. Take the energy that you need to revitalize you and then let the rest flow back down to its source, returning it to the earth.

The Festival of Osiris:

The Festival of Osiris was performed on the first new moon in the month of March, before the Spring Equinox. It is a festival that celebrates the entry of Osiris into the moon, or the rise of his Night-time sun from his realm in the Underworld.

The fructifying energy of the increasing lunar moon was linked to the fertility of the land. As a Divine Nature God, Osiris would sail through the heavens in his barque to be reborn as the moon each month in a twenty-eight day cycle of birth and death. This same number, not so coincidentally, as the twenty-eight years, that he ruled Egypt as King.

The ritual itself is a re-enactment of myth, much like all the formal rituals of the Temple. It can be done outside under the new moon or in your sacred space.

Ritual Checklist:

Natron water
Ankh
Crook and Flail
Osiris incense
Silver altar cloth
Crescent shaped planter
Potting soil
Corn seeds (one for each participant)
Water bowl
Parchment Paper or Papyrus
Ritual Time: New Moon, 9:00pm

The Osiris ritual, is begun by purifying the temple area with Natron water and Frankincense. The altar is covered with a silver cloth. A white and green candle, representing the moon and Osiris respectively, are lit. Also placed on the altar are the Ankh, the Crook and Flail and the crescent shaped planter. The Osiris incense is lit in the Thurible. Each participant has prepared ahead of time a petition to Osiris. One side of the petition carries the hieroglyph of Osiris while the other side contains their petition or will. The petition should be one of bringing new things into a persons life, or starting a new project or life's path.

This ritual is followed by the serpentine procession lead by the High Priestess. As in the Isian ritual in the previous chapter and any other formal Egyptian ritual, the sistrum purification is performed at the entrance to the temple. When this is done and the participants have entered the temple, the High Priestess leads the meditation. The elemental deities are invoked:

East, Neith: "Hail thou that ruleth the east, Lord Duamutef, jackal headed son of Horus, Neith warrior goddess and protectress come forth from the abyss to lend your presence here."

West, Selkit: "Hail thou that ruleth the west, Lord Quebsennuf, falcon headed son of Horus, Selkit scorpion headed goddess of magic come forth O' soul of the Ram of the West."

North: Nepthys: "Hail to thou that ruleth the north, Lord Hapi, ape headed son of Horus, Nepthys, goddess of the underworld, come forth from the lands of rebirth at the mouth of the Nile."

South, Sekhemet: "Hail to thou that ruleth the south, Lord Imsety, human headed son of Horus, Sekhemet lioness of the desert who guards the eternal flame. Come forth from the red land of the Uraeus."

After the elemental invocations, the High Priest in the place of Tehuti leads in an invocation to Osiris:

Tehuti: "Osiris Per Aha! Come forth as the nighttime Sun, to be reborn again as the silver moon whose rays shineth upon the waters and the fields and the minds and bodies of men. May your soul journey in the barque of Maat through the stars of Orion!"

Osiris: "I come forth from the Land of The True Voice, Amenti, the west. My journey has been long, but I have not been idle."

Isis/High Priestess: "What gifts have you brought back from your journey?"

Osirs: "I have gathered the seeds of immortality and rebirth from the dark fields of my realm in the Duat. I offer them to the children of Kemet."

Isis: "O' my Lord, we accept mightily these sacred seeds, but ask that you infuse them with your Khu energy."

Tehuti: "Place the Ankh to his lips so he may receive the Breath of Life!"

The High Priestess as Isis places the Ankh to the lips of Osiris with her right hand, her left hand is raised to channel the energy of the moon.

Isis: "Receive this Breath of Life my Lord and husband."

Tehuti: (to participants) "Children of the Gods, do you have anything that you would place as an offering to the Bright Shining One?"

At this time each participant comes forth to place petitions into the thurible on the altar.

Isis: "Will you Bless these seeds my Lord?"

Osiris breathes on the seeds and places them one by one into the crescent-shaped planter, there is a seed for every participant. By then the petitions have burned to ashes and the High Priestess sprinkles them over the planted seeds.

Isis: "The hopes of humankind reside in your shining being. Your body is scattered upon the sacred land of Kemet so that it may nourish all life."

The High Priest brings forth a pitcher containing blessed water, he pours it over the seeds.

Tehuti: "Receive this life giving fluid! May these seeds rise like Osiris to reach up to the heavens of the Un-Nefer. May this grain feed the children of the Land."

All Say: "Rise, O' rise Osiris, shining Lord of Eternity and Everlastingness."

Tehuti: "Let us now celebrate the rebirth of our Lord."

The Neters are dismissed, starting in the east:

East: "Return, return O' Lord of the east Duamutef, jackal headed son of Horus, Neith,

warrior goddess sheath thine arrows in the land of the abyss."

West: "Return, return O' Lord of the west Quebsenuf, falcon headed son of Horus, Selkit goddess of magic return to the land of your birth"

North: "Return, return O' Lord of the north, Hapi, ape headed son of Horus, Nepthys goddess of the underworld, return to your watery realm."

South: "Return, return O' Lord of the south, Lord Imsety,

human headed son of Horus, Sekhemet lioness of the desert return to your vigil of the eternal flame."

The beer and bread is shared and the temple is opened.

The Djed Pillar of Prosperity

The Djed pillar was often a popular amulet of prosperity in ancient Egypt; Its color was most always green, and amulets of it were made of various materials from Faience, a type of ceramic to malachite or turquoise and even gold itself.

Magically, the Djed pillar was referred to as the 'Backbone of Osiris' or the 'Still Heart', most likely an association with stability. And what could be better than financial stability! In this spell we will create a magical prosperity amulet of the multi-faceted Djed pillar so that, just as its pillar grew to gigantic proportions so shall our prosperity.

What you will need:
1 Green candle
1 Gold candle
Magnetic gold sand
Green Fimo clay
Osiris Oil
Lotus bowl filled with purified water
Ritual time: The full moon

On the night of the full moon, when it has risen full and bright, most usually at 9:00 pm; begin by forming your Djed pillar out of the green clay. When you have finished, sprinkle some of the magnetic gold sand over it and bake the clay in the oven for the prescribed time. While your amulet is in the oven place the Lotus bowl filled with the purified water outside in the moonlight to absorb the lunar rays. When it has baked to the prescribed hardness, remove it from the oven and let it cool. Bring the bowl of water back inside. With the little finger of your right hand, anoint your Djed amulet with the Osiris oil, from top to bottom. As you do say these words:

"Osiris, thou who hast passed through The Disk, receive this perfume, may it purify you in Un-Nefer, the land of Amenti."

Next, dip the anointed Djed into the water. As you do say these words:

"The holy waters of the Nile, the influx shall bring prosperity and all things of the land, to feed my needs. I myself am pure and worthy of these gifts, AU A AB KUA NETERI KUA."

Your Djed pillar amulet is now complete and will serve you as a magical conduit for attracting prosperity and abundance. Make sure to carry it with you always!

The Scarab of Success

In the previous chapter, we touched briefly on the symbolism of the Scarab, the dung beetle that was revered as the god of rebirth, Khepera. Each day he was said to push his solar ball across the sky to give light and warmth to the earth, bringing about the renewal of life. The dark sun of Osiris that was reborn each month from the underworld, could not be born without the help of the Sun.

For how could there be moonlight without the illumination of the Sun? In Egyptian Magic the energies of Osiris and Khepera were often used together, these two energies working through and for each other to bring about renewal and rebirth.

The Scarab was a very popular and versatile symbol. It was largely used as an amulet for almost every need under the sun! Heart Scarabs were placed over the heart of the mummy so that the heart of the deceased would be reborn in the afterlife. Scarab amulets were worn for magical purposes to bring in prosperity, success, and love. A giant stone scarab located by the sacred lake at the temple of Karnak was purported to bring fertility to women who wished to conceive.

Scarab amulets were made of various different materials: gold, carnelian, malachite, faience, jade, lapis lazuli, and many more. The Scarab of Success that we will use for our spell can be made

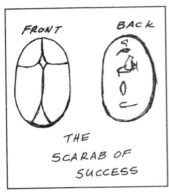

out of self-hardening clay or Fimo, in the color green, to bring growth and prosperity to a new project. You will need to create it ahead of time so that it will be ready on the day that you wish to perform the spell. To create your Sacrab form a small oval with a rounded top and flat bottom. Inscribe the following hieroglyphs on the back.

What you will need:
Frankincense
Cinnamon Oil
Pomegranate seeds
1 Gold candle
Fenugreek seeds
1 small green bag
Ritual time: Sunrise

Begin this spell at sunrise, the day you wish to start a new project, the day that your success is desired. Purify your working space with Natron in all four corners. Then anoint your scarab with the cinnamon oil, front and back, taking care to trace the hieroglyphs.

Inscribe your desires on the gold candle, using a pin or small knife. Then anoint the candle as well. Place seven fenugreek seeds into the green bag. Now take the Scarab, bag and candle to the east. As the sun rises over the horizon light your green candle. Hold the scarab up to the rays of the sun. As you do say these words:

Io tabao, sokhom-moa, ohk-ohk-khan-bouzanou, aniesi, Ekomptho, ketho, sethori, thmila, aloupokthri.[2] Let every thing that I shall apply to my hand today, to happen.

Repeat this seven times then place the scarab into the bag with the fenugreek seeds. Carry the bag with you always, until you attain your success. Let the candle burn all the way down.

Spell for Making the Body Whole

This next spell makes use of a magical doll or poppet, created in the image of the person who has requested healing. I emphasize 'requested' because you may not do magic to heal someone without their permission. Why is that?

Because, in the magical practices the ancients believed that illness started in a persons spiritual mind. And illness was often part of a karmic path. The sick person would often go to a priest or priestess to receive the divination or dreams needed to reveal the source of their illness. Once the information was revealed to them, they could request a healing or spell to make them well.

What you will need:

1 roll or block of white or natural beeswax
Red embroidery thread
Local honey
Lotus Oil
Licorice
Powdered Myrrh
Osiris incense
1 small square of white cotton or silk
1 red candle

Ritual time: Midnight of the full moon

To begin this spell, you must start when the first light of the moon has risen, usually 9:00pm.

Hold the wax in your hands to soften it. When it has begun to soften somewhat, you can start molding it into a small mummy-shaped doll. Make sure to emphasize the sex of the doll. When you have finished shaping it, you can add some personal affects such as a lock of hair or fingernail clippings from the person wanting to be healed. Press them into the softened wax. Then carve out a hole where the heart of your doll should be. In a bowl, mix a tiny amount of the licorice, myrrh and honey to form a paste. Carefully fill the heart-hole with it. When that is done, light the red candle. Look into the flame and say these words:

"Behold, Osiris, the flame of the fire-eater Sekhemet. May you steady her mighty hand to bring the AB of _____ (persons name) into the light of Purification."

Then drip the red wax from the candle into the heart-hole of your doll until it is filled.

Place the candle aside. Next, anoint your doll with the lotus oil starting at its head. Recite the prayer for healing:

I have purified the body of _____(persons name) may he/she be healed of all illness and negative energies. May the body of _____(persons name) be made whole, its vessel and Sekhem restored. 'He/she who hath come into existence in the image of the gods' XEPERU EM NETER HAU."

When you have finished, place it on the white cloth where the moonlight can shine on it overnight. In the morning, wrap the doll in the white cloth, then bind it tightly with the red thread. Place it on your altar until the illness disappears.

CHAPTER SIX

Horus and the Temple of Edfu

"The Light shall prevail over darkness."
Inscription on the temple wall at Edfu

The Lord of the Heavens

The ever-constant, omnipotent Sun that dominates the Egyptian sky is the realm of the king of the solar deities; Horus/Her, the falcon headed god whose piercing eyes represent the sun and moon.

Horus first appeared in Egyptian history during the pre-dynastic times as a Creator God. A being of mysterious origins, he was known as 'He Who is Above'. His first seat of worship was in the Delta region of Upper Egypt. There, Horus was linked with the pharaoh Naquada III, O dynasty, as a god of kingship. When the two lands of Upper and Lower Egypt were united, he became The Lord of Two Lands, the god whose strength had unified both realms. Early depictions of Horus as a falcon with a snake in his talons can be seen on a the palette of Narmer, the pharaoh whose triumph in battle brought about the unification of the north and south, the upper and lower lands of Egypt.

On an esoteric level, the concept of Horus as the Sun/Creator placed him like Ra, as the representation of the Creator force. The other gods and goddesses were then seen as aspects of that Creator Force.

For example: Isis, Osiris and Tehuti, the Shemsu-Hor, who emigrated as settlers to the Nile Valley, the predecessors of the so called Master Race, were worshiped as the 'Followers of Horus'. They were identified as the disciples of the Creator. Emissaries of the Gods come to earth, who by their very example in the Dynasties to come, became earthly gods in the form of Pharaohs and were referred to as the Living Horus. Thus, these pharaohs became representations of the Gods on earth, whose powers and privileges allowed them to rule supreme over other mortals.

The earliest concepts of Horus were as the Father God, Horus/Ra. Ra represented by the disk of the sun and Horus the celestial falcon became the transmutation of that solar energy. Throughout Egyptian history, Horus morphed into a variety of forms constantly regenerating, like the great fiery star itself. In fact all the aspects of Horus are related directly to the phases of the Sun, or the solar phases.

Re-Herarkty: Horus the Elder, the Face of the Sky by Day, is depicted as a falcon-headed man with a solar disk on his head. He was responsible for all creation and rose each day on the eastern horizon as the scarab god Khepera. His daily journey across the sky was honored in temple rituals at dawn, noon, dusk and midnight.

Her-Mem-Akhet: As Horus of the Horizon, he was the earliest representation of Horus ever in the form of the Sphinx at Giza. The Sphinx represented the sun at dawn and, in turn the dawning of the Egyptian civilization in the age of Leo.

Her-Sa-Ast: Horus the Younger, the young son of Isis and Osiris, signified the first feeble rays of the morning sun. Young and untried he personified the innocence of youth. He is the winter born sun, whom Isis gave birth on December 23rd, the Winter Solstice. In this aspect, he was often depicted as an infant or youth suckling at his mother's breast or as a young boy wearing a side-lock of hair.

Horus of Edfu: Heru-Behudeti, Horus of the Midday Sun, it is here that Horus is in his most powerful incarnation as the Warrior Priest and Avenger of Darkness in the form of Set. He is depicted in this aspect as a falcon-headed man wearing the double crown of upper and lower Egypt. He holds a mace in one hand; all-powerful, as he smites the enemies of Egypt. He is the personification of the Egyptian Hero. Likened to the Greek Apollo, Horus was thought of as handsome, charming, and possessing of refined skills such as a beautiful voice and artistic talent.

The Four Sons of Horus: The four sons of Horus, are better known as the gods of the Canopic jars, those sacred funerary vessels held the internal organs of the deceased, and were thought to have been the children of Horus by his mother Isis. The Four Sons of Horus represent the four cardinal points, the four elements, and the four energies of the body used in Egyptian healing. They are as follows:

Duamutef: Jackal headed god, ruled the East, the lungs and the element Air.

Qebsennuf: Falcon headed god, ruled the West, the liver and gall bladder and the element Earth.

Hapi: Ape headed god, ruled the North, the small intestines and the element Water.

Imsety: Human headed god, ruled the South, the stomach and large intestines, and the element Fire.

The battle of light over darkness

The most popular and illustrative myth surrounding the god Horus is most assuredly the story of how he avenged the murder of his father Osiris, and regained the throne of Egypt.

It all started when Isis gave birth to Horus in the papyrus marshes of Khemmis. At the time of the Winter Solstice, alone on the island of Buto, in the Delta region of Egypt, Isis gave birth to a sickly infant struggling, that was born prematurely, and who struggled to survive in the dangerous company of scorpions and crocodiles. When at last he grew to manhood, he went with his mother to the council of the gods, the great Enead. Here he spoke of the cruel murder of his father and of the treacherous way in which his uncle Set had seized the throne. The council agreed that Horus was the rightful heir to the throne by all, except of course, the evil Set. Set then challenged Horus to a battle, for the throne of Egypt.

This battle, between the golden son of Osiris and his uncle the beast-headed Set was to take place outside the papyrus marshes. At first, Set suggested that they transform themselves into hippopotami, in this form they would then dive down as far as they could and the first one to return to the surface of the water would be the winner. Fearing for the life of her son, Isis threw a copper harpoon into the water to kill Set. It struck Horus instead and he leapt from the water. Set fled into the marshes, only to creep out again that night. He transformed himself into a serpent. When Horus was sleeping he bit him in the eyes, he then tore them out and flung them into the swamp, where they fell, two beautiful, lotuses bloomed.

As Horus lay bleeding against the trunk of a tree, the goddess Hathor, the Lady of the Southern Sycamore, found him. Noticing that he had been blinded, she transformed herself into a lioness. In her lion form Hathor went out into to the desert where she found a gazelle and milked it. She then took the milk back to Horus and bathed his eyes with it. As she dripped the milk into the wounds, she spoke magic words over him. The pain began to recede and Horus was healed, his sight restored to him.

In the form of a hawk, Horus flew out to avenge himself upon Set. Seeing this, Set transformed himself into a fish and leapt into the Nile. Horus transformed himself into an otter and swam after his Uncle. Rising from the water, Set transformed into a swallow. Horus, in his hawk form once again, gave chase. As Horus gained swiftly on him, Set spied a field of grain and transformed himself yet again this time as a tiny piece of grain. Horus was not to be defeated. Thusly, he transformed himself again as well, this time as a duck that ate the grain that was Set. He triumphed over his uncle, regained the throne of his father Osiris. The seed of evil was devoured and light shone upon the land.

Magical Attributes:

Name: Horus, Her, Her-Mem-Akhet, Re-Herarkti, Horus of Edfu, Her-Sa-Ast, Harpoctrates.

Symbol: Falcon, The Wejat or All Seeing Eye

Color: Yellow and gold

Planet: Sun

Metal: Gold

Number: 2

Tools: The Winged Disk

Herbs: Horehound, blue lotus

Key words: Warrior, Savior, Oracle, Avenger, Lord

Edfu

March 16th 2000, 12:00 noon

Every time I arrive at this temple, the sun is at its zenith, a cosmic conspiracy for sure! But whatever it is, it never fails to make me wonder if the sky is just a little more of a celestial blue here, or if the sun is just a little higher in the sky than usual?

We approach the vast complex of Edfu, from the north, walking along an endless expanse of the stone wall that surrounds the outer courtyard. When at last we turn in to the front hall of the temple, we are confronted by; two fierce eyed stone statues of the Horus falcon who guard the entrance. Ever vigilant, they stand as sentinels, protecting the southern portal which leads to the domain of Set the Destroyer...

Edfu, domain of the Warrior Prince

The temple of Edfu remains today as one of best preserved, intact examples of the ancient Egyptian temples. It is also the only south-facing temple in the land as well. The placement of this temple, as with all the 'Houses of the Gods'; is directly related to the magical attributes of its specific deities. This temple is said to have been built upon the very battlefield where Horus battled his uncle Set, avenged his father's death, and to claimed the throne of Egypt.

The original temple was built by the infamous magician/architect, Imhotep, during the reign of Thutmosis III in the 18th dynasty. It was reconstructed and re-dedicated in the Ptolemaic times—first, by Ptolemy III in 237 BC, and finally finished by Ptolemy XII Auletes, also known as the father of Cleopatra VII.

The story of Horus and all his glory begins at the towers of the great entrance pylons. Here identical mirror images of the god depict the scene called the 'Feast of the Beautiful Meeting' in which Horus of Edfu is united with Hathor of Dendera as his wife

This symbolic meeting was played out in ancient times, when for a period of thirteen days, once a year, the priests and priestesses from each temple would visit each other amidst feasting and celebration.

Once past the pylons of the grand courtyard, is the entrance to the temple, which is guarded by two black basalt statues of Horus. Above the doorway is his symbol, the winged disk. The temple itself is supported by huge pillars, carved in the composite, floral style of the Ptolemaic period. On every wall is depicted the story of Horus, the 'Drama of Edfu', which details

Horus' battle with Set for the throne of Egypt. In scenes from the drama, Set appears as a Hippopotamus. Horus, depicted as a young king spears him with a short blade.

This drama was performed by the priests each year, It was called the 'Festival of Victory', where Horus would systematically pierce the body of Set using ten harpoons, starting with his snout and continuing down his back. At the end of the drama a ritual cake baked in the form of a hippopotamus would be eaten, thus completing the total vanquishing of the enemy Set.

In the very back of the temple is the sanctuary. Inside that small rectangular room is a red stone shrine. The shrine housed the solar barque, which would in turn carry the anointed statue of the god during ritual procession. On either side of the sanctuary are individual rooms dedicated to various gods and goddesses. Towards the front of the temple, on the west side, is one of the most significant and mysterious rooms of all, the Oil Room. This room was the magical oil laboratory of the priesthood. It was here in which the priests were trained in the art of Oil Magic the early predessesor of aromatherapy. Its walls are covered with oil recipes for both magical and medicinal purposes. Some of the plants specified in the recipes are rare and extinct - such as the blue lotus. A duplicate of this Oil room we will see later in the temple of Dendera.

The next place of interest is located outside the temple proper, the mummisia. It is here in the privacy of the 'Birthing Room of the God', that we have decided to do our ritual...!

Dedication to Horus

There is a very special energy that radiates from the walls of this sacred birthing room. It is dark and womb-like, the skylights shedding very little light. The walls are covered with scenes of the birth of Horus.

Our ritual today will be one of dedication, in which we will dedicate ourselves in our hearts to be one with Horus. We will sacrifice our concerns of the earthly plane for a higher purpose in our lives that of courage, self-sacrifice, and familial love. In doing so, our BA soul will take on the power to soar like the hawk and to reach unimaginable heights.

Ritual Checklist:
Lotus Oil
Sistrum
Horus statue
Pure white cloth
Bread
Wine

After making sure we will be undisturbed during our ritual, we first create a temporary altar by placing a white cloth placed in the center of the stone floor. On the altar is arranged the Horus statue, the bread and wine, and the anointing oil. The sistrum purification is performed by a priestess, on each person, and followed by three deep Sekhem breaths. We observe a moment of silence in which we visualize ourselves soaring high in the sky like the hawk flying across the sun. When we have achieved the waking meditative state I begin the invocation.

High Priestess: "Horus, Per Aha, Lord of the Two Lands, Heir of Eternity, Come forth from the solar disk to open our two eyes, NEFER ANKUS NEB MERT!"
Participants:
"Hika,
Hika
Hika
Hika
Hika!"
High Priest/Horus: (holding up the lotus oil) "Behold! Here is the evidence of my sight, the perfume of my being!" He then

places the bottle of oil against his forehead, blessing it. A priestess comes forth and takes the blessed oil. She then anoints each of the participants in the third-eye area.

High Priestess: "O' Horus, we thank you for this sacred oil, the effluvium of your birth. May it open our eyes. May the strength of your eye be in us. May you rise each day strengthened like Ra, may that strength be in us, may we see as you do, what is only Right and True."

The statue is then taken from the altar and presented to High Priest/Horus.

Priestess: "Horus, we dedicate this statue to you. In your likeness it shall be purified. May it live as a symbol of your strength and everlastingness."

Horus: "This perfume has made me whole, my strength returns with the Disk, I am ready to do battle against those who would upset the order of the Sekhem Ur, 'Great Sekhem' of which all life revolves around."

The Statue is then passed to the High Priestess, she anoints it with oil and passes it to the other participants. When the statue has been anointed by all present it is held towards the light.

All say: "Pure is thy Sekhem, pure is thy Ka, pure is thy soul in the land of Amenti."

The statue is then wrapped in the pure white cloth to be carried with us. The next morning it will be put in a place where it can catch the first rays of the morning sun.

Before we leave the mummisia we take time to thank the gods with a libation of bread and wine.

Invocation to Horus:

The power of Horus takes flight with the first rays of the morning sun. So it would only seem fitting, then, that an invocation to him should be spoken at sunrise. The magic of Horus is solar magic, which gains in power steadily through the day as the sun reaches its zenith. All the phases of the sun hold significance for a Sun

God. The Dawn is a time of new beginnings and creativity: Noon or Midday the height of the solar energy, which can give a powerful boost to all magical works especially healing. Dusk is a time for reflection and divination and Midnight a time to cast off unwanted things in your life. The ancient Egyptians worked with both the sun and the moon, coordinating the phases of both to do potent magic works.

This invocation to the falcon-headed god calls forth the power of the sun to energize you and all your magical workings. An invocation designed to bring new life into a new project, a special health need or simply to give you a boost to start your day.

Ritual Checklist:
1 gold candle
Milk
Bread
Dragons Blood incense
Natron water
Horus statue
Lotus oil

This ritual is best begun in the early morning, a few minutes before dawn. First, as always, you must take time to purify your ritual space. Sprinkle the Natron water around your working space, sunwise starting in the east. Follow that with the Dragons Blood incense. When you have finished, set up your altar or table facing the east. Place upon it your Horus statue, the gold candle, a small bowl of milk, and a plate of bread. Anoint your statue with the lotus oil. If you do not have a statue, you can use a framed picture of Horus and anoint the glass of the frame.

Wait silently in contemplation until the first rays of the sun appear over the horizon. Light your gold candle. As the sun gets brighter take five deep Sekhem breaths. As you breathe visualize the golden light of the sun entering your lungs and filling your body. Using a vibrant voice, much like a chant, begin your invocation.

"Horus Per Aha, come forth this day as the Divine Hawk, Re-Herarkty, Maat Heru.

Come forth this day to maketh my body whole, to purify me, to nourish me and to establish a place for my Khu among the beings of radiant light.

The god Tem shall take you up in his boat and you shall rise as Khepera, to be reborn in another form.

Your wings will cast shadows on all doubt and fear.

Your eyes, the twins of fire, will see through all obstacles put in my path.

The heavens will open this day for you so that it may transform my will into being.

Horus, your breath is within me.

Horus is upon his seat, I have risen like a hawk divine!

HERU HER NEST F, AU A XAA KUA EM BAK NETERI"

When you have completed your invocation you should feel invigorated, ready to take on your day. Let your candle burn all the way down and leave the offerings of bread and milk on the altar until dusk.

Astral Travel Ritual

Not only did the Egyptian believe that the soul had many aspects, but that it could travel about at will. Astral travel and shape shifting were a part of the magical repertoire of the priest or priestess of the temple. Many passages in the Book of the Dead allude to the transformation of the soul into animals, such as a hawk a swallow. These winged creatures were able to fly into the realms of the heavens and effectively travel into other dimensions.

In this ritual, we will be using the universal Egyptian symbol for time travel, the winged disk which is also a symbol and tool of

Horus the Divine Hawk.

The first steps of this ritual should be attended to very carefully. Astral travel is an advanced technique and must be approached with responsibility. Make sure that you are in a place where you will be undisturbed for this ritual. There are definite dangers in being interrupted during astral travel. The Astral umbilical cord, a cord that connects the astral body to the physical body may be damaged or severed, which could in a worse-case scenario result in illness or shock.

Ritual Checklist:
Winged Disk
Cedar oil
1 blue candle

To prepare for this ritual, you must first take a purifying Natron bath. To create your Natron, use the formula of ½ cup of salt and 3 tablespoons of bicarbonate of soda added to your bath water. Relax into your bath, letting the tensions of the day drain away. When you are finished with your bath and have dried off, anoint yourself with the cedar oil. Anoint yourself on your forehead, and between your eyes- the third eye area. Anoint the soles of your feet, your palms, and the middle of your chest on your heart chakra center. Put on a loose robe to wear. Find a comfortable place to lie down either on a bed or a couch, even the floor will do. When you have chosen a comfortable place to lie down, hang the winged disk on the wall or ceiling at eye level so that you will be able to see it clearly without straining. Light the blue candle so that its flame may serve as a beacon to which the Ka may to return to safely.

The next step is to lie down, with your arms by your side. Breathe deeply and evenly. As you breathe concentrate on the center of the winged disk. Feel the energy of your body lifting up higher and higher like a hawk. Continue to concentrate on the center of the disk, until all images that surround it disappear. Your Ka is lifting higher and higher. You fly directly into the center of the disc. Space and time are as one. As your astral body hovers above, you can see your physical body as it lays there. At this time many things could be revealed to you, past and present even things of the future. However, if at any time you feel that your astral body is starting to 'rush' or you feel a sensation of pins and needles in your limbs begin to bring your astral body back into its physical vessel. To do this, visualize the silver cord, the astral umbilical cord, which connects the Ka and the Khat (physical body). Begin to pull the cord in through your Ab or heart chakra center, closer and closer until your astral and physical body are one again.

Wejat Protection Spell

The Wejat or Udjat eye symbolizes the Eye of Horus, that which was restored to him whole by Hathor and Tehuti. A powerful protection symbol, The Eye was often placed above the doorways of houses and tombs to ward off evil. The Wejat was seen as two types, one eye facing right and the other facing left, representing the sun and moon, Ra and Osiris respectively. In Egyptian magic today, the Eye of Horus was used for protection, healing, and the 'sending away' of negative energies.

In this spell, we will be creating a magical talisman using the Wedjat eye. As with any talisman it should be created for a specific purpose: To ward off gossip at work, to prevent negativity with a neighbor, and so forth. When the talismans purpose has been achieved, it is either burned or buried so that it cannot pass into unwelcome hands.

Ritual Checklist:

1 red candle
Horus statue or picture
Dragons Blood incense

Wejat oil: Patchouly, Dragons blood, Myryh, Lotus,
   Frankincense, Neroli, Cedar
1 4" x 4" square of papyrus or parchment paper
Black ink
Ritual time: Full Moon, 9:00 pm

On the night of the full moon, prepare your ritual space by first purifying it with Natron water, followed by a thorough censing with the Dragons Blood incense. Using the black ink, draw a Wedjat eye on one side of the piece of paper and inscribe the following hieroglyphs on the other side.

When you are finished, anoint the talisman with the Eye of Horus oil. On the red candle, inscribe those things that you would wish protection from, using a pin or a small knife. Then anoint the candle with the oil as well. Place your candle and talisman next to your statue or picture of Horus. Light the Dragons Blood incense and pass your talisman through the smoke seven times. Then light the red candle. Picking up your Wejat talisman 'show' it to the flame by holding it up so that the candlelight illuminates it from the back. As you do say these words:

"The Eye of Horus, Maat Heru, has risen to conquer all that would harm me.
   It has cast light where there is darkness,
   It has brought renewal like the Bennu to all that failed me,
   It makes me see clearly all that would be harmful and
      injurious to myself and my loved ones,
   MAAT MAN HAPEPET MAAT."

Then place your Wejat talisman under the red candle and let it burn all the way down. The next day, you can put your talisman where it will do the most good, such as above your door or in your car. When that purpose has been served remember to destroy your talisman by fire, or by burying it.

The Amulet of the Wedjat Eye

In this next ritual you will be making an amulet using the symbol of the Wejat, the left facing eye, the lunar eye. This magically created amulet can be carried or worn on your person, or even placed on your altar to add to the 'Hikau' or magical energies of your sacred space.

Traditionally, Wejat amulets were made of precious and semi-precious materials such as gold, hematite, carnelian and the most desired of all- lapis lazuli. If these materials are not available, which they most probably won't be, you can always fall back on self-hardening or Fimo clay to create your amulet.

The optimum time of the year to create your amulet is the Summer Solstice, when the sun is at its zenith. A Wejat Eye, created in the height of the solar energy will possess great strength, protection, and healing powers.

What you will need:

Self- hardening or Fimo clay
Powdered Horehound herb
Wedjat Oil
Dragons Blood incense
1 piece of red silk
Blue and gold paint
1 piece of papyrus or parchment paper
Black ink
Natron water
Ritual time: Noon, the day of the Summer Solstice.

The first step in creating your Wejat amulet starts with the purification of your 'secrets', or magical ingredients. Begin by passing the clay, silk and parchment through the smoke of your Dragons Blood incense seven times. As you do say these words:

"I purify thee, O' emblem of the Divine Hawk. May you be made ready to receive the Neter Aaa."

Next sprinkle a little of the Natron water on the ingredients, and let them dry completely. When they are dry it is time to form your amulet from the clay. A good size is approximately 2 ½ inches long by 1 ½ inches high. When you are finished, bake it in the oven according to the directions.

The next step in the creation of your Wejat Eye is to write the 'Spell of Creation' on the papyrus or parchment paper. Write it in black ink, followed by the appropriate hieroglyphs.

The Spell of Creation

"I have come forth as a Shining One,
A creator of light from the body of Khepera,
I have been born from the horizon,
A lion god, the son of Isis.
All things shall be created from my body, every living thing,
For I am Horus The Divine Hawk that dwelleth in the splendor of the heavens, ANKUS UTA SENB."

After you have written the spell, set it aside. Take your amulet out of the oven and let it cool completely. When it has cooled, paint it first gold then blue for the center of the eye. Put your spell into a small fireproof dish and burn it into a fine ash. As the smoke rises recite the spell in a resonant voice. Add seven drops of the Wejat oil to the ashes, along with a tiny pinch of the horehound herb. Anoint your amulet with the ash mixture and place it where it can absorb the noonday sun. Leave your amulet there until the next day. Then wrap your amulet in the red silk until you are ready to wear it or carry it with you.

The Amulet of the Ladder

The amulet of the Ladder was a curious magical object that became popular in the Middle Kingdom. Most often found in tombs, it represented a ladder, the ladder that assisted the deceased in their ascent to Heaven. It was believed by the Egyptians that the Neteru, the gods, dwelled high above on a rectangular plate of iron. This iron plate was supported at all four corners by pillars that represented the four cardinal points. According to myth, Osiris himself had difficulty reaching the iron plate and had to be assisted up the ladder by Horus. The Ladder therefore, stood for spiritual assistance and support. In the form of an amulet, the Ladder can be used for magical help of all kinds. In the case of illness, the Ladder can be carried or worn to banish the sickness itself. For money matters, the amulet can be carried to ensure that money will multiply and not be lost. It can also be used to overcome a confrontation or a court case. By its very symbolism, the Ladder will prop up and enhance most any of your magical workings.

In ancient times the Ladder amulet was made primarily of wood and sometimes an ancient faience porcelain. For our purposes, we will call on the magical self-hardening clay! This way we can make the ladder small enough to wear.

(Insert Illustration #54 here)

Ritual Checklist:

Self- hardening or Fimo clay
Kyphi incense (used to invoke the Egyptian gods)
1 gold candle and 1 white candle
Lotus oil
Ritual time: Full moon, 9:00 pm

On the night of the full moon, prepare your amulet in the usual way. Form a small ladder shape ½" x 1" out of the clay and put it in the oven to bake according to the directions. Then, anoint the candles with Lotus oil. Inscribe the hieroglyph for Horus on the gold candle and leave the white one representing the 'Great Unknowingness' blank. When your amulet is completed, anoint it also with the oil and place it between the two candles. Light your Kyphi incense and your candles, starting with the gold one, raising your hands in the Ka position invoke the power of Horus:

"Hail to thee, O Horus, Mighty one of Ra,
Extend your help to me in all matters,
May I have the extra strength of fire,
The fire from Maat Heru, the Wejat eye,
To overcome my obstacles, to see where things are hidden,
To add power to my magic!
Hika, Hika, Hika, Hika, Hika"

Leave your amulet between the two candles until they have burned down completely. When you are ready to use it, your Ladder amulet can be placed on the altar to add additional 'Sekhem' to your work.

CHAPTER SEVEN

Hathor and the Temple of Dendera

"Let me eat my food under the sycamore tree of my Lady Hathor, and let my times be among the divine beings who have alighted thereon.

In a clean place I shall sit upon the ground beneath the foliage of the date,

Palm of the goddess Hathor, who dwelleth in the spacious disk as it advanceth towards Annu."

The Egyptian Book of The Dead

(Insert Illustration #55 here)

(Insert Photo #19 here)

The Great Mother of the World

The goddess Hathor can be identified as the earliest Mother Goddess concept in ancient Egypt. The roots of her worship can be found as far back as the pre-dynastic cow cult where she was revered as a Cow Goddess of fertility. In that primitive capacity, she was identified with the fertility and abundance of nature, which included crops, vegetation and all animals.

Evidence of this first incarnation can be seen in some of the archaic and pre-dynastic art such as the pallette of Narmer; where Hathor is portrayed in dual images, at the very top of the pallete, as a woman with a cow head and ears with curled horns. These curled horns; such as depicted on a pre-dynastic urn from Heirakonpolis, symbolized lunar crescents; the stars inside and on the ears, represent Hathor's Sky Goddess aspect. The precursor of her later role as Patroness of Astrology.

Her name, Het-Hert, meant House of Horus, and she was thought to be both the mother of Ra and the wife of Horus. As mother/daugher and wife of the sun, it signified her association with the phases of the moon and a woman's menstrual cycle.

As the cow goddess Mehurt, she was the dark night sky that protected Ra/Horus within her ample bovine body until he could be reborn again each day. In such aspect she was also the reviver of the Solar Eye, and was sometimes referred to as the female Ra or Raet who nourished the gods for their journey through the various realms of the underworld. In this multifaceted capacity, Hathor was seen as giving birth to the sun, mating with the sun and nurturing the sun.

Popular throughout Egyptian history, Hathor/Het Hert acquired a myriad of identities both as a local and a national deity. As a goddess of duality, she was sometimes called the 'Lady of Two Faces'. As the perfect example of Egyptian womanhood, depicted cow headed with a solar disk or as a beautiful woman wearing the vulture headdress. Her bovine aspects encompassed fertility, domestic virtues, mother daughter relations and childbirth. As a beautiful woman she was likened to the Greek goddess Aphrodite the patroness of love, romance, beauty, adornments, perfumes, sex and joy.

There is however, a darker side of Hathor, one that was leftover from a more primitive time, where she is portrayed as a lion-headed woman wearing the solar disk and the Ureaus on her head. Hathor The Avenger, who according to myth killed so many of the king's enemies that she became empowered with the blood of men. When Ra learned of this he feared that she would destroy the rest of humankind. He sent messengers post haste to Elephantine to bring back large quantities of mandrake root. He then mixed the root with some of the slain men's blood and put it into the beer supply. He ordered seven thousand jars of the blood-beer. It was then placed where Hathor had chosen to slay the rest of the men. Ra ordered the servants to flood the fields with beer stating 'I will deliver mankind out of her hands'. When Hathor came across the flooded fields she saw her reflection in the liquid and feeling pleased drank deeply of it. She became so drunk that she was no longer able to complete the slaughter of humankind.

The Seven Hathors

In keeping with her standing as a goddess of the people, Hathor had seven aspects of herself that were worshipped at her main temple at Dendera. They were the seven Hathors from seven individual Nomes or territories throughout Egypt. Their images, carved on the walls of the temple show them as young women playing tambours and wearing the solar disks on their heads. The names of these seven goddesses were: Hathor of Thebes, Hathor of Heliopolis, Hathor of Aphroditopolis, Hathor of Momemphis, Hathor of the Siniatic Peninsula, Hathor of Herakliopolis and Hathor of Keset.

Why were there so many names and associations for this beloved goddess of the common people? What was their purpose? In myth, the seven Hathors acted like handmaidens or disciples to the premier goddess, Hathor of Dendera, acting upon the people's wishes in all things. She represented to them all things that were sacred to womanhood, the personification of creation, the wife and consort of the living son/sun Horus.

Magical Attributes:

Name: Hathor, Het Hert, Hathor of Dendera, The lady of the Southern Sycamore, The Golden One

> Symbol: Falcon inside a house or box, Cow wearing a lunar Disk and Menyat necklace
>
> Color: Apricot, Orange, Black
>
> Planet: Uranus
>
> Metal: Copper
>
> Number: 6
>
> Tools: The Mirror of Hathor, Menyat Necklace, Sistrum
>
> Herbs: Sycamore, Myrtle, Rose and Sandalwood.
>
> Key Words: Love, Romance, Astrology, Music, Dancing, Fertility and Beauty.

Dendera March 18th, 2000

After driving mile upon mile through rustic farmlands and exausting all the showtunes that we know, we finally reach Dendera in the middle of the afternoon. The goddess must truly be smiling upon us, for we find ourselves nearly alone at this great temple. I make the suggestion to Amr that we do a brief tour of the Temple before our ritual, as a way of attuning ourselves with the goddess energies, energies that fairly seep from the stones as we approach the silent halls.

In a meditative state, we enter first into the Great Hall, the inner hall and finally the inner sanctuary. I can almost hear the whispers of the priestesses as they go about their duties, smell the ancient incense, and feel the strength of the magic that has gone before me.

Entering Dendera, we are captivated. As if we are entering into a great web of feminine power where interwoven strands reach out to all levels of humanity, space, time and beyond...

Ewn-Net-T-Neter, City of the Feminine Principle

In no other temple in Egypt can the essence of the feminine principle be felt so strongly as the temple of Hathor at Dendera, referred to the ancient Egyptians as Ewn-Net-T-Neter, City of the Feminine Principle.

This temple, which was originally called Tentyra, the Sacred City of the Three Temples, started out as just that, a religious site that contained three small temples. The sanctuary of Hathor, the sanctuary of Horus, and the sanctuary of their son Ihy, of which, very little remains today.

The origins of the main temple of Dendera go back as far as the first dynasties of the Old Kingdom of Khufu and Pepi I. Rebuilding of the temple took place as well during the New Kingdom under the direction of such famous pharaohs as Thutmosis III, Amenophis III and the great Rameses II. However, the temple of Hathor that stands on this site today was rebuilt and refurbished during the Ptolomaic and Graeco-Roman periods.

The façade of the outer hall of the temple is like no other found in Egypt, in fact the whole temple itself exudes a sense of fantasy and whimsy in its design. The 24 columns that support the ceiling are carved into four-sided sistrum shaped pillars. The face of the goddess depicted as a woman with cow ears is repeated on all four sides.

On the ceiling of the great hall, decorated in beautiful original colors, is a perfectly aligned chart of the heavens, complete with the signs of the zodiac and the sky goddess Nut swallowing the sun. As you traverse further into the inner hall of Dendera, the incredible complexity of the Temple of Hathor begins to reveal itself.

Though originally dedicated to the Goddess Hathor, Dendera is a temple dedicated to all goddesses. Inside the sanctuary are shrines allotted to a variety of goddesses, some of them so obscure that representations of them have survived only on the walls of Dendera.

The foremost inner sanctuary is dedicated to Hathor; it is referred to as the Hwt or womb of the temple. It is here in the inner sanctuary that the stone shrine that held the statue of the goddess and her visiting barque were placed. On all sides, lining the walls of the inner sanctuary are chapels for a variety of other goddesses as well as the two rooms reserved for the 'Attributes of Hathor' the Sistrum and the Menyat necklace. Behind the central shrine, at the very back of the sanctuary of the goddess, is a most curious place. A shrine for the 'Hearing Ear'. This shrine, in the form of a niche in the wall, backs up to an opening in which the priestesses would listen to a person's petitions and prayers to the goddess. Much like the confessional in the Catholic church!

Underneath the walls and floors of Dendera are located secret crypts in which the treasures of the temple were stored, such as the statue of the Ba of Hathor. Chief among these chambers is the Crypt of Nectanebo, the magician Pharaoh. It was here that Nectanebo I, the last native Egyptian pharaoh, would practice his magic. Many years later, Queen Cleopatra VII, was to perform many of her own magic and rituals in this crypt as well.

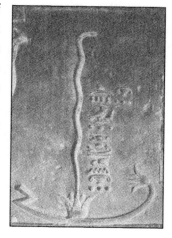

The next area of interest after leaving the temple proper, are the special chapels located on the roof. These chapels can be reached by a narrow stairway to the west of the offerings hall. Lining the wall of the staircase is a detailed carving of a procession of priests and the king ascending to the roof carrying the statue of the goddess. The carvings are so lifelike that they make you feel as if you are part of the procession yourself!

Once on the roof, there are several small goddess chapels, which were used for various rituals throughout the year; such as the 'Resurrection of Osiris' and the celebration of the 'Birth of the Solar Disk'. The most famous of these small temples, is the Astrological Temple. This is the temple that featured the 'Zodiac of Dendera' a detailed carving of the Egyptian zodiac fashioned like a round wheel held and up at the four cardinal points by different gods and goddesses. The original ceiling was removed by Napoleon Bonaparte in the nineteenth century, and ironically, it's a copy of the original ceiling that hangs there now!

As fascinating as the temple itself are and the outbuildings of Dendera. To the west of the temple is the sacred lake, one of the best-preserved in Egypt. The lake is dry now, but evidence of ground water can be found at the bottom by means of a subterranean staircase.

Last, but certainly not least, are the birthing houses and the Sanitorium located to the west of the temple as well. The Sanitorium dates from the Greaco-Roman period and is one of the most intact examples of one to be found of any of the Egyptian temples.

Hathor was a goddess of compassion and her sanitorium was always open to the sick that were in search of healing. Inside the sanitorium there are many individual chambers for patients who would seek the help of the priestesses. Here they would be treated with herbal and magical medicine and receive help from the gods through healing dreams.

The Birth Houses, or mummisia, of Dendera are; the Roman

Birth house, the Ptolomaic Birth house and the Temple of the Birth of Isis. The mummisia of Dendera, just like the mummisia at the Temple of Isis, is where the celebration of the Birth of the God takes place. Here at the temple of Hathor it is the birth of her son Ihy by Horus of Edfu. This ritual birth was celebrated as a temple event and often featured the current reigning pharaoh as the Divine Infant.

It is here in the exquisitely beautiful Ptolomaic Birth house that we have chosen to do our Hathor Ritual of Abundance...

Hathor Ritual of Abundance

The Ptolomaic birthing room is a small enclosure with the sky as a roof and desert sand for the floor. Even in its state of partial ruin it fairly pulsates with energy! The walls of this mummisia are covered with some of the most exquisite and rare carvings of all the remaining temples in Egypt. My favorite carving is wrought in delicate lines on the northwest wall. It depicts the frog headed goddess Heket placing an Ankh to the baby pharaoh's lips, giving him the 'Breath of Life' as he is born from the center of a lotus flower.

Right from the beginning, from the time we had stepped over the threshold, all of us felt as if we were standing in the very womb of nature, surrounded by vivid representations of the goddess in all her glorious aspects.

This day, in this sanctuary of birth, we will be performing a ritual of abundance to Hathor in her aspect of 'Great Nourisher and Comforter'. The abundance that we will work for will not be limited to the mundane, but will instead relate to all levels in our lives, spiritual, emotional and physical.

Ritual Checklist:

Sistrum
Hathor statue
Red wine

Dates
Bread
Frankincense
Thurible
Chalice
Lotus oil
Parchment or Papyrus paper
Black ink
Flowers

Our altar today will be a pure white cloth placed in the center of the room. The altar will be set with a statue of Hathor, flowers, bread, wine, dates, ritual chalice and the thurible. Petitions to the goddess have been prepared ahead of time. These petitions, in the form of tiny scrolls, are written in black ink on parchment paper, each of them is anointed with a drop of lotus oil.

Two of the priestesses open the ritual by performing Sistrum purifications, as I consecrate our space with the incense. When that is done, the Hymn to Hathor is repeated.

High Priestess/Hathor: "Hathor, Lady of Amentet, Dweller in Urt, Lady of Ta-Sert, The Eye of Ra, Dweller in his Brow. Face beautiful in the boat of a million years. The seat of peace for doing what is Right and True among the favored ones, you have been reborn to make the bark of the sun great, to sail forth the right and true!"[1]

After the recital of the hymn, the Sistrums are shaken five times to send the words out to the Neters (the gods).

Priestess: "O' Hathor, Great Nourisher, I have traveled these many miles, across desert sands. I thirst and my body is weak."

The High Priestess/Hathor takes the wine and bread off the altar and offers the priestess a small amount.

Hathor: "Come, take nourishment for thy body, so that the vessel of your Khat may be strengthened."

A second priestess then comes forward.

Priestess: "O' Hathor, my heart is filled with sorrow and unrest."

A ripe fig is then taken from the altar and offered to the second priestess.

Hathor: "Partake of this fruit of love so that your Ab shall be comforted with the radiance of love."

A third priestess then comes forward.

Priestess: "O'Hathor, what use is there for the strengthening of my Khat and Ab, my body and heart, if the radiance of my soul is dimmed?"

Hathor: "The fire of your Sekhem has need of nourishment, come forth and receive the 'Breath of Life'."

The High Priestess then places the Ankh to the third priestess's lips, sending her the Sekhem energy.

Hathor: "The Divine Radiance is housed again within your vessel, you shall not want of anything, earthly or otherwise."

The sistrums are shaken and everyone joins in to say these words: "Maati" (right and true).

At this time everyone has a chance to come forth and place their scrolls into the thurible, as the smoke of their burning rises into the air the sistrums are shaken once again to send their messages to the Unefer.

High Priestess/Hathor: "Hathor, Het-Hert receive now these offerings, and with them our thanks, for you have brought comfort and nourishment where there was a void. We pay homage to you O'beautiful Golden One. We are now strong in the living as well as in the realms of Amentet."

The wine and bread is shared at this time. Afterwards, we will all join in a procession carrying flowers and the ashes of our offerings to the sacred lake where we will place them in the waters.

The Ritual of the Beautiful Meeting

An Egyptian Wedding Ceremony

In a magical society like ancient Egypt, many of their rites of passage were patterned by the example of their gods. This especially holds true in the case of the Pharaoh, the royal family and even the nobility, for they alone could stage a ceremony in the grand manner befitting of the gods.

One of the most popular of these marriage themes was the 'The Feast of the Beautiful Meeting' the marriage of Horus the Sun God to the Goddess Hathor.

In ancient times, this ritual would take place in the spring, in the month of May. It would begin on the new moon with the goddess Hathor leaving her temple to embark upon the journey to her husband's temple at Edfu. Amidst cheering and festivities, her statue would be loaded onto a golden barque. In this golden boat she would sail upstream for over one hundred miles to the city of Edfu where they would be met by the equally golden and magnificent barque of Horus. In order for their marriage to be fortuitous the two boats had to arrive at the same time. On this day of the new moon the priests and priestesses of each temple would greet each other and music, dancing, and feasting would take place.

The sacred couple would retire to the chapel for their private ceremony, celebrating the day of the 'Beautiful Embrace' their symbolic mating. A mating that would bring fertility to the land and its people much like a Beltane or May Day celebration.

Horus and Hathor would spend a total of thirteen days together. On the day of the full moon Hathor would have conceived of their son Ihy and was ready to sail back to Dendera.

The Wedding Ceremony

The ancient Egyptian wedding ceremony has much in common with many pagan and even modern day middle-eastern weddings.

In this wedding ceremony, the man is given the option of a real wedding, or what was called strangely enough, 'a Year of Eating' in which he was basically handfasted for a year to determine if the women he had chosen, could bear children. Both bride and groom would draw up contracts stating their properties and specific vows they would make for their marriage. These contracts would be presented at the ceremony. After the wedding, the bride would be expected to go to the groom's house. To 'Be with him in his House' a phrase that doesn't leave much to the imagination but hopefully was good for both of them!

Ritual Checklist:

A statue or picture of both Hathor and Horus
Sistrum
Menyat necklace
Red Candle
Frankincense
Hathor mirror
Chalice
Lotus bowl
1 small loaf of cornbread baked in a conical shape
1 ceremonial earthenware jar (the sacred vessel) with lid (AB)
Anointing oil (Lotus, Ylang Ylang, Sandalwood, Neroli, Frankincense, Myrrh, Rose)
Wreaths made of flowers for wedding party
3 necklaces made of rosebuds
2 red cords, each with thirteen knots, one knot for each vow, each day of Hathor's journey
Wine
Washbowl and towel
Ritual time: 2:00 pm on the full moon

Note: The Egyptian bride traditionally wears red with a wreath of flowers in her hair preferably blue lillys. Her Menyat necklace is carried in her right hand in the traditional way. The man wears white, usually a loose fitting robe-like garment. Both are encouraged to add their favorite Egyptian adornments.

To begin the ceremony, the temple area must be purified in the usual way. First with Natron water, then with incense, starting in the eastern quarter and moving sunwise to the south, west and north.

Four people are needed to represent the goddesses of each quarter along with the priestess and her handmaiden.

After the temple area is purified and consecrated, the handmaiden performs the Sistrum purification on the High Priestess, the goddesses, then the bride and groom and the other participants. The High Priestess then in turn performs the Sistrum purification on the handmaiden. The participants are led into the temple. The goddesses of the quarters enter the temple in order. Finally, the handmaiden leads the bride and groom into the temple to stand before the altar. She carries the conical corn cake and sets it upon the altar.

The altar is set up with flowers, god and goddess, candles, anointing oil, sacred vessel and chalice along with each of the elemental representations. At the base of the altar are placed a washbowl, towel and vessel of purified water.

When the incense and candles are lit, the High Priestess then opens the ritual by raising her arms in the KA position.

High Priestess: "May this temple be now consecrated in the presence of the Divine Lady Hathor Netert and before the gods and goddesses of the great Enead. May we gather now for this sacred ritual of love with these two that wish to be wedded.

_____and _____

come forth now and stand before us and the Un-Neters."

The bride and groom are asked to come forth to stand before the altar. They are then asked to remove their shoes so that the handmaiden can wash their hands and feet to symbolize the purity of their union.

The remaining water is poured into the sacred vessel on the altar.

Starting from the east, the goddesses that represent the elements come forth to take their symbols from the altar.

East/Neith: "Hail thou that ruleth the east Lord Duamutef, jackal headed son of Horus, Neith warrior goddess and protectress come forth from the Abyss."

West/Selket: "Hail thou that ruleth the west, Lord Qebsennuf, falcon headed son of Horus, Selkit scorpion goddess of magic come forth O'soul of the Ram of the west."

North/Nephtys: "Hail to thou that ruleth the north, Lord Hapi, ape headed son of Horus, Nephtys, goddess of the underworld come forth from the land of rebirth at the mouth of the Nile."

South/Sekhemet: "Hail to thou that ruleth the south, Lord Imsety, human headed son of Horus, Sekhemet, lioness of the desert who guards the eternal flame, come forth from the land of the Ureaus."

High Priestess: "Hathor, Per Aha! I invoke thee O' Golden One, Mistress of Love, Divine daughter of Ra, Mother of grace, whose crescent crown doth shine as a star, through eternal space, from whose womb all creation has sprung,

May your stars illuminate this man and woman who wish to be wedded,

So that they may see into their hearts and the love that they hold for each other.

A AU PEST EM A PERT!"

The Sistrum is then shaken five times upon the invocation.

High Priestess: "Have you contemplated on the state of your marriage? And have you lived, worked and meditated together? Do you still wish to be wedded?"

After the couple give their answers, they are asked to present their wedding contracts. The wedding contract consists of 13 vows and pledges made to each other and could include dowry items as well.

After the presentation of the contract the High Priestess takes the two, knotted cords from the altar.

High Priestess: "The words of your contract are the bolts that hold the temple of your union together. They are Maati, the Right and True of what is contained in your heart. These cords are yours to keep as a symbol of those words, each knot a magic word spoken in the ears of the Gods, the shining ones of the Un-Neter."

The bride and groom are then asked to kneel before the altar, the man to the right and the woman to the left. The handmaiden binds the right wrist of the groom to the left wrist of the bride with the red cords.

High Priestess: "With love lying in your hearts and minds I ask you now to choose the state of your union. From the coils of the serpent Tiamet you must choose of the Earth, Heaven or the Duat so that once chosen your love will blossom forth as the red lotus from the waters of Nu."

The couple chooses one. The handmaiden then presents the anointing oil to the couple.

High Priestess: (to groom) "If you truly desire at this time to be wedded to this woman, I bid you let your beloved anoint thee upon thy brow with sweet perfume."

The bride anoints the groom on his forehead with the oil, and in turn the groom anoints the bride on her forehead.

Groom: "Accept from me my beloved this pledge, that my life and love shall be forever in your service, I ask you to accept me for that which is mine shall be yours also."

Bride: "My love I accept your pledge of love, for thou knowest what is in my heart as I know what is in thine, I will come to thee in thy house and the magic of my will shall ever be yours."

High Priestess: "If thou_____(brides name) does truly desire to be joined with this man, I bid you present him with a vow."

Bride: "Accept my word as my treasure, Maati for all the gods to take note of. I pledge all that is mine in the name of my Lady Hathor so that our love shall flourish as the lotus and papyrus of the in the Waters of Life."

Groom: "My lady, I accept your pledge of love as I accept the Right and True of your words, for thou knowest what is in my heart as I knowest what is in thine."

There is silence for the space of five heartbeats.

High Priestess: "Spirits, Neteru, if there be any that object to the union of these two souls give us a sign."

High Priestess: "In the name of Hathor, Isis and Amon Ra and all the gods of the Enead, I ask that you guide this woman and this man on the path they tread as they become one in the eyes of the spirits and the earthly world."

The couple is then helped to rise. The High Priestess holds her ankh to the groom's lips.

High Priestess: "_____(grooms name) will you take your beloved into your house as your wife? Comfort her in times of health and in sickness? Vowing to hereafter to treat the flesh, mind and soul of your new mate as that of your own for as long as there is the radiance of love between thee?"

High Priestess: (placing the ankh to the brides lips) "_____(brides name) will you provide your beloved with the comfort of your body, the nourishment of your foods and the perfume of thy being. Vowing to treat the flesh mind and soul of your new mate as that of your own as long as there is the radiance of love between thee?"

After the bride and groom have given their answers the groom breaks a piece off of the corn cake and feeds it to the bride.

Groom: "The fruit of the fertile fields shall be yours in this symbolic loaf. A symbol of my steadfastness and ability to provide."

Groom: "I _____take thee_____beloved daughter of Hathor and Isis into my house to be my wife to love and cherish as long as there is love between us."

Bride: (feeding groom the cake) "I _____take thee_____beloved son of Hathor and Isis to be my husband and cherish as long as there is love between us."

The High Priestess pours wine into the chalice and offers it to the bride who shares it with the groom.

Bride: "Just as Horus beheld the face of his goddess radiant with love, as he lay under the sycamore tree, so shall you behold mine and accept from me this sweet nectar of life. My flesh to your flesh, my soul to your soul, it is my will to become as one with you."

The groom drinks from the chalice and repeats the vow: "My flesh to your flesh, my soul to your soul, it is my will to become as one with you."

The handmaiden steps forth and presents the sacred vessel to the bride and the purified water to the groom. The groom pours the water into the vessel.

Groom: "Osiris, great father and bringer of life bless the fluid in this symbolic AB vessel, may it hold transformation and everlastingness."

The vessel is returned to the altar and the bride and groom exchange rings, gold for the man and silver for the woman. As they do they say these words:

"In the name of Hathor and Isis and all the gods of the Enead we pledge love, truth and friendship for our lifetime, in this world and beyond."

High Priestess: "Now as the gods have witnessed this rite I proclaim that you are husband and wife. May you go forth as strong and as swift as the waters of the Nile, and that all that ye shall leave in your wake shall produce beauty and sweet perfume upon the land. This work of joy born upon the lips of Nut, is done, yet like the birth of the sun, only just begun. May the love that has led you to this bonding be forever growing and flourishing. Ankus, Uta, Senb!

Hail to thee O'mighty Hathor,
Hail to thee O'mighty Isis,
Give your blessing upon these two.
Hika!
Hika!
Hika!
Hika!
Hika!"

The bride and groom may kiss at this time. Sistrums and Menyats are rattled and it is time for feasting and dancing.

Hathor Love Spell

When it comes to matters of romantic love and passion Hathor, the Lady of Sensual Delights, reigns supreme. It was her breath among the sycamore trees, that stirred the gentle breezes, that fanned the flames of lover's desires. It was she that fed them dates and sweet honey cakes to renew their strength. The consummate deity of love, Hathor was everything that was sensual, passionate and sweetly perfumed. Love spells and rituals done in her name carried with them a special potency.

This particular love spell makes use of a wax figurine molded in the shape of the intended lover.

Ritual Checklist:

1 sheet of white or red beeswax
Avocado oil
Red thread or string
Thirteen needles
Myrrh oil
Hathor incense
Ritual time: Waxing moon.

On a Friday night during the waxing moon take up your beeswax and mold it your hands until it softens. Then begin to form it into the shape of your intended love interest, making sure to exaggerate the genital areas.

When that is done carve his or her name on the head or neck region. Then carve the name of Hathor and her hieroglyph on the ribcage area. Anoint your doll starting at the head with the avocado and myrrh oil. Next tie knots in the red string, as many as you would wish the spell to last. Wind the knotted string around the doll, then light your incense. As you do say these words:

"Oh Hathor, great goddess of the House of the Face, who reigneth over love and beauty, Oh, Nourisher of Man, may the love of _____(lovers name) be for me as the hunger of a starving man for bread and sweet wine.

Your next step involves the needles, so very Egyptian that it could have come straight out of the crypt of the Necatanebo himself!

When you are ready, take up your first needle pierce the head of the doll, as you do say these words: "May the thoughts of _____(lovers name) be only for me"

With the second needle pierce the eyes, "May the sight of _____be filled only with me".

The third needle pierces the nose, "May the nostrils of _____be filled only with the scent of me".

The fourth needle pierces the mouth, "May the speech of _____be filled only with my name".

The fifth needle pierces the heart, "May the love of _____(lovers name) for _____(your name) reside always in the breast of_____(lovers name)".

With the sixth and seventh needles pierce both arms, "May the love of _____be always open to me, embracing me with love".

The eighth and ninth needles pierce both hands, "May the hands of _____be ever ready in the service of me".

With the tenth needle pierce the abdomen area. If the figurine is female pierce the womb area, for a male pierce below where the navel would be. Say these words accordingly: For a woman, "May the womb of _____ be ever fertile and ready to receive my seed". For a man, "May the fire of Amon Min lay ready in the hips of _____ to produce for me your seed of life".

With the eleventh needle pierce the genital area. For a woman: "May the vagina of _____ be ever ready to receive me".

For a man: "May the phallus of _____ rise strong as a stallion only for me".

Finally with the last two needles pierce both legs. "May the Menti(legs) of _____ stand solid like a pillar to support our love."

When at last your figurine has been pierced in all the right places, pass it through the incense smoke to perfume it. Then place it in a hidden spot where your lover will be sure to pass by, you can even put it under your bed!

The Menyat

One of the most mysterious tools or attributes of Hathor is the Menyat necklace. This tool was made of rows of beads that formed a collar with a long paddle shaped counterbalance. It can be seen depicted in many of the Egyptian art and sculpture, gracing the throat of countless goddesses and queens of ancient Egypt. A piece of ritual jewelry, much like a 'Jewel of Art' it was either worn around the neck or carried in ones hand like prayer beads. During ritual, it was often shaken like a sistrum to send out the words or songs of power.

The magical properties attributed to the menyat were those of joy and health and the merging of the male and female energies, similar to the Yin and the Yang concept. The goddess Hathor herself, was referred to as 'The Great Menyat' because healing and medicine, particularly aromatherapy, were taught to the priestesses of Hathor at Dendera.

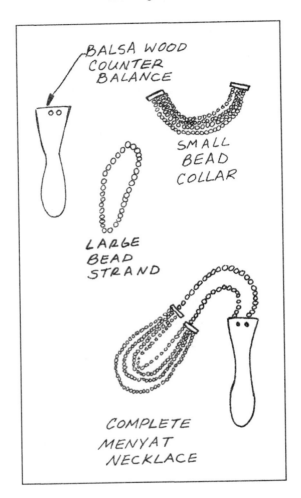

Construction of the Menyat

To create your own Hathor tool of art is very simple, and like all your Egyptian tools can be personalized with colors and symbols. This special magical object, is a very specific 'attribute' of Hathor and is used primarily by women. It is used to channel and send out the power of the goddess, it is also used for meditation and healing. The beads of the Menyat when lightly swished over a person's body will drive out disease.

The Menyat, in ancient times, was made of gold and semi-precious stones usually malachite, lapis lazuli, turquoise or carnelian. Those materials if not available may be substituted with colored beads. The paddle or counterbalance can be constructed out of balsa wood from a craft or model store.

What you will need:

Colored glass beads ¼ to ½ in diameter
Cord for stringing beads
1 rectangular shaped piece of balsa wood 3" x 9"
Gold paint
Wood carving tool
4 small brass jewelry rings

The first step in creating your Menyat begins with the shaping of the counterbalance. Using the wood-carving tool begin to shape the bottom of the rectangle in the following way:

The next step is to string the beads. Begin by stringing the small beads in four strands so that they lay just at your collarbone. Attach them at each end to the small brass jewelry rings. Attach them in turn to one row of larger beads. Then string each single strand of the larger beads from the brass ring to the counter balance to at the top.

The Amulet of the Menyat

The Menyat like the scarab was a popular amulet of the living as well as the dead. Made primarily out of the sacred malachite stone, it was carried or worn as a charm to promote healing and good health. It was placed on the mummies as well for the same reason, only for the Afterlife instead.

For the construction of our Menyat amulet we will be using the 'new' Egyptian substance again. Self hardening or Fimo clay.

Ritual Checklist:
Green Fimo clay

Lotus Bowl
Green candle
Ankh
Rose and Lavender buds
Photo of yourself or of a person needing to be healed

Construction of your Menyat amulet should begin during the waxing moon, with the preparation of the sacred blessing water. To start, pour purified water in to the Lotus bowl. Make the sign of the Ankh over the bowl, as you do visualize a golden light infusing the water.

"May you be as pure as the waters of NU, a fluid of creation and transformation!"

Then sprinkle the rose petals and lavender buds into the bowl. Then place it outside in the moonlight to allow the herbs to steep. While the herbs are steeping, it is time to form your amulet out of the clay, taking care to put the Menyat symbol on one side and the hieroglyph for health on the reverse. When the amulet is complete, it is ready to be consecrated in the blessed water. To do this you must submerge it completely then say these words:

"Oh Hathor, you have perfumed thy waters with the sacred plants of healing.

In this fluid I place your holy attribute, the Menyat so that all that comes in contact with it shall be whole in their body and their KA spirit,

ANKUS, UTA, SENB!"

Remove the amulet from the water and dry it. Then anoint the candle and the amulet with the Lotus oil. Light the candle and the Hathor incense. Take up your amulet and using the red string bind it face to face with the photograph of the person you wish to heal. Then pass it through the incense smoke and say these words:

"The vessel of _____(name) is purified,

The vessel of _____(name) is strong,

The vessel of _____(name) is healthy,

The vessel of _____(name) shall rise like Bennu from
   the flames"

Your Menyat amulet, must then be wrapped in the red cloth and placed next to the candle. The candle should be allowed to burn all the way down. For as the candle flame burns, so shall the life force of the sick person be renewed. Later, when it has burned all the way down, you can unbind the photo from the amulet. Your amulet can then can be worn or carried for extra protection.

Spell for Making Merry The Heart

There were strong beliefs surrounding the heart in ancient Egypt. They considered the heart to be the center of the spiritual being. Much like the Native American belief that a person 'Thought through their Spiritual Heart'. That was considered by the Egyptians to be Maati, the Right and True of a person. Subsequently, when a person's heart was unbalanced through heartache, health issues or disappointment a spell for making the heart feel happy was needed.

Ritual Checklist:

   1 small yellow pouch
   1 small piece of turquiose
   Red string
   Hathor oil
   Powdered Henna
   1 small piece of parchment
   Black ink
   Kyphi incense

On the night of the waxing moon, begin your spell by first

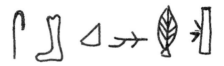

inscribing the hieroglyph for happiness on the piece of parchment. When you are finished, roll it into a tiny scroll, tie it with a piece of red string then anoint it with the Hathor oil. Place it into the little yellow bag.

Add the Henna and the piece of turquoise. Close your charm bag tightly.

Next light your Hathor incense. Take up your charm bag and pass it through the incense smoke three times. One for each coil of the serpent, the Earth, Heaven and the Duat. As you do so, say these words:

"Homage to you, O' Lady of the Sycamore,
Your sweet perfume purifies my heart,
The light of your disk nourishes it,
I am filled with happiness,
My heart will not feel pain,
My heart will live in the Right and True, the Maati
Make merry my heart! Fill it with light and joy!
A ua Pest em A Pert!"

At this time pick up your Sistrum face the west and shake it five times to send your words out to the goddess. Place the bag around your neck so that it is even with the Heart Chakra.

Divination with the Hathor mirror

The Mirror of Hathor, as I described in chapter two is a copper disk in which one side is highly polished and one side is scoured. The highly polished surface is the one we shall be using for our divination. If you do not have a Hathor mirror the same results can be accomplished with a magic or black mirror.

This divination is best performed in the dark of the moon, that time between times, the night before the new moon, the dark abyss of the Duat. A time when Hathor, in her guise of the cow goddess Mehurt, readies herself to give birth to the sun, a rest period, in which she gathers around her all the wisdom of the stars and the moon.

Ritual Checklist:
Hathor Mirror
Mugwort oil and herb
Kyphi incense
1 purple candle
Cakes, wine or grape juice

The first step in preparing for your divination starts with the anointing of your mirror with the mugwort oil. Mugwort is a strong visionary herb that is used for psychic receptivity and dream work. Mugwort oil is quite rare and you will probably have to order it from an herb specialist. You can also make your own Mugwort oil by using the Egyptian method of oil extraction detailed in the Temple Ethics chapter of this book.

To anoint your mirror, use the pinkie finger of your right hand. With a small amount of oil trace a circle around the edges of the mirror. Place the purple candle off to one side then light it. Make sure that the candle flame is not shining directly into the mirror but instead casts a luminous glow on the copper surface, for it is here in this glowing surface that your images will appear. Take three deep, Sekhem breaths, then when you are ready invoke the spirits of the mirror.

"O' Hathor thou art dark as the invisible darkness, dark as the Duat.

O' Lady of the West, Mehurt Great cow goddess of the place of mystery and rebirth,

Where Osiris cometh from,
Bring forth that shining light from your womb,
So that I may divine all that the gods have to reveal for me."

After your invocation, sit for awhile in silent contemplation, and watch the candle glow on the surface of your mirror. You will see it cloud over slightly then recede. Your images will now begin to appear. Open your mind and relax.

When you have finished, cover your mirror with a dark cloth. Partake of your bread and wine remembering to leave aside a portion for the nourishment of the spirit of the mirror.

CHAPTER EIGHT

Sekhemet and the Temple of Karnak

Homage to thee, O'Sekmet-Bast-Ra, thou mistress of the Gods, thou bearer of wings, thou lady of the red apparel, Queen of the crowns of the South and North, only One, sovereign of her father, superior to whom the gods cannot be, thou mighty one of enchantments in the boat of a million years..."

The Egyptian Book of The Dead

The Flaming Eye of Ra

In the land of ancient Egypt, Kemet a land of extremes in all things, nature, birth, death abundance and starvation,  veangance and mercy, one goddess rides the razors edge, her name is Sekhemet the lioness and she is the personification of creation and destruction.

The origins of this powerful goddess, Sekhemet/Sekhet, are mysterious and obscure. Her very name traces its roots back to one of the most fundamental concepts of Egyptian spirituality, The Sekhem, or vitalizing life force within, the very 'Fire' of life.

The appearance of Sekhemet as a leonine deity can be traced to the birth of the land of Egypt as it first appeared in the age of Leo. The Sphinx itself was painted red in ancient times and its leonine body bespoke of her fierce protective qualities.

Once again we can refer to the Narmer palette from the first dynasty where two lions, with curious serpentine necks entwined, represent the two lands of upper and lower Egypt.

Proof positive that Sekhemet 'The Powerful' was among some of the earliest God concepts and like Horus, Ra and Hathor, she reflected attributes of them all.

As an aspect of Ra she stood for the sun's fire, his 'Flaming Eye' whose solar power had the ability to create and destroy all life. An aspect in which she was often depicted as a lion or a lion headed woman with a sun disk upon her head encircled by the red Ureaus Serpent. As an aspect of Horus the son, she was the lion of the desert. The Warrior Avenger of the enemies of Egypt. Pharaohs invoked her power as they drove their chariots into battle, including the most famous warrior pharaoh of all time, Rameses II, who declared himself to be 'Born of Sekhemet'.

In her Hathor aspect Sekhemet was even more of an enigma. Where Hathor was gentle and beautiful, a comforter and provider, Sekhemet in contrast, was the dark side of the goddess, representing the fierce uncompromising force of the mother lion that protects her cubs. She is the Unmerciful One, who slew the enemies of Ra and became drunk on their blood. Thus, Sekhemet/Hathor was a goddess of love and war much like the Norse goddess Freya who drove a chariot pulled by cats. Subsequently when the horse and chariot were introduced to Egypt in the 14th dynasty Sekhemet merged with the Syrian goddess Ashtoreth and took on the name of Mistress of the

Chariots or the Lady of Horses.

The primary associations of Sekhemet though, were as a solar deity, which in itself identified her as an ancient goddess. Some of the earliest Egyptian temples ever built, such as those of Memphis and Heliopolis, were temples of the Sun. It was there that Sekhemet was worshipped as the 'Great Cat' or Nesert (flame) Lady of the Flame. One depiction of Sekhemet was a two headed lion- with one head facing east and the other facing west symbolic of her control over sunrise and sunset and all the phases of the Sun.

As the personification of fire, Sekhemet's power extended not only to the eradication and destruction of evil forces, but to the destruction of disease as well. Sekhemet was the patron goddess of the Sekhemet Priests, the surgeons of ancient Egypt. The power of her healing flame (the Sekhem) was used in secret magical rituals to bring healing to the living and the dead, and to purify and invigorate the soul in the Afterlife.

In the Old Kingdom Sekhemet was identified as the 'Beloved of Ptah', the wife and counterpart of the Divine Mason, the creator god Ptah. Together with their son Nefer-Tem they formed the Memphis triad of Ptah-Sekhemet-Nefer-Tem. Later, when the infamous scribe and healer Imhotep became deified, he became known as the son of Sekhemet as well.

The Serpent from the Abyss

One of the most interesting relationships surrounding the lion goddess is her association with the red Ureaus snake or the Royal Cobra. The word Ureaus was derived from the Greek word 'Uriaos' which meant 'She who rears up'[2] . The name represented a fiery serpent that spits flame from the eye of Ra. This serpent could be invoked as Sekhemet to

come forth as a terrible force to vanquish the enemies of the Right and True.

In Egyptian mythology, the original sky god was a primordial god who possessed a single eye. When he wept from that eye, the tears that fell to earth created the people and animals of the earth. One day, when the two children of the god became lost he sent his only eye out into the Abyss to find them. While the eye was gone another eye grew upon the god's face. The original eye returned with the god's children only to find itself replaced. It became so enraged, that the primordial god transformed it into the cobra Mehenet which became the serpent goddess aspect of Sekhemet. In that form, she sat coiled and ready, upon the brow of the god to guard his crown. Although the red Ureaus serpent gave the god great power and magic, it could never really be satisfied. It remained an unpredictable, combustible force like the Sun and the lioness Sekhemet herself. Symbolism of this myth would suggest that the Ureaus could be seen as the 'Fire of Sekhemet', the Sekhem Flame contained within the Creator. That flame which animates all life, and the fertile seed of fire that is born from the serpentine, feminine principle.

Magical Attributes:
Name: Sekhemet, Seket, Nesert, Mehenet
Symbol: Lion, Sphinx, the Sekhem, Spitting Cobra
Color: Red
Planet: Sun
Metal: Gold
Tools: The Papyrus Scepter, Arrows, Knife
Herbs: Pomegranate, mandrake

The Temple of Ptah-Sekhemet at Karnak
Nestled behind the sanctuary of Montu, at the north gate of the vast complex of Karnak, lies the temple of Ptah-Sekhemet, a tiny temple, no more that three chapels and a courtyard. The courtyard

is filled with curious offering tables, tables clearly designed for the 'Wet offerings' by virtue of the draining grooves carved into them. They stand as silent testimony to what was assuredly a place of blood sacrifice to this fierce warrior goddess. A worn stone staircase leads up to the roof of the temple where the solar rituals were performed.

Oriented east to west, the original temple was built by Thutmosis III. It was refurbished though both during the Ptolomaic and Roman periods. The three chapels are reached through a series of five gateways, leading to a small hall in which lotus capitals flank their gated entrances. Two of the chapels are dedicated to Ptah and the third, located on the southernmost wall, is dedicated to Ptah's consort, Sekhemet. Here inside the darkened chapel stands a magnificent statue of the lion headed goddess, which miraculously, has survived untouched from ancient times.

Karnak December 29th, 1998

Dressed in red to honor the Lady, we enter the small, darkened chapel of Sekehemet. A guard fortified with the appropriate 'Baksheesh' agrees to keep the curious away.

Upon entering the narrow stone chamber, a magnificent sight is revealed before our eyes, a lifelike statue of Sekhemet herself, carved in delicate regal lines of solid black basalt. Cleverly placed under ancient skylights she is illuminated with the golden rays of Ra himself. She stands upright with a Lotus scepter in one hand and an Ankh in the other. The expression on her face is benevolent, fierce, yet merciful at the same time.

It is here at her feet that we will lay offerings and petitions in preparation for the powerful healing ritual that we will perform this day.

Nesert Ritual of the Blue Flame

I believe that it is truly a testament to the power of Sekhemet that her statue has remained untouched throughout thousands of years. Some say that they fear even now to disturb such a power. Whatever the reason, her statue is surely a conduit for the great magic that is Sekhemet. Here in her small chapel with the doors closed, with only the light of candles and ancient skylights, it is like entering into a time capsule. Your senses remember the sound of ancient music, the scent of temple incense and the radiant force of the goddess.

The ritual that we will perform this day will awaken the Sekhem force of the goddess so that it may heal ourselves, and our loved ones. We have prepared beforehand, healing petitions written in red Dragons Blood ink, on small squares of parchment. These healing petitions contain the name and the healing wish of a person either for themselves or a loved one. During the ritual, these petitions will be consumed in Sekhemet's fire.

Ritual Checklist:
Thurible (incense burner)
Sekhemet incense
Pomegranate juice (The Blood of Sekhemet)
Photos of loved ones
Petitions
Candles

Dragons Blood incense
Temple Dancer, Najla

The temple is first purified with the Dragons Blood incense. Then a priestess performs a sistrum purification on all who have entered the sacred space. I begin the ritual with an invocation to the Mighty Lioness herself.

High Priestess: "Sekhemet, Per Aha, Mighty Lady of Flame, Beloved of Ptah, guardian of the Flaming Eye or Ra, I invoke thee and beseech thee to lend us your Sekhem power and strength, for this ritual of great healing."

All say:
"Hika,
Hika,
Hika,
Hika,
Hika."

The Sistrums are now shaken five times, then it is time for the meditation.

High Priestess: "Let us now take five Sekhem breaths."

Visualize your feet rooted to the earth like the pillars of the temple. From the base of the pillar, from the abyss below, you can see a blue flame. Bring that flame up your spine, spiraling it in a clockwise motion.

At this time, our temple dancer Najla puts on music and begins the sacred dance, an ecstatic dance designed to raise the Flame within each of us. I ask each person to place their right hand on the left shoulder of the person next to them to form the links of a serpent. When this is complete the blue flame is sent in a clockwise direction from person to person. At the head of the serpent is the High Priestess.

High Priestess: (extending her hands towards the statue of Sekhemet, thumbs forward) "Sekhemet Nesert, Keeper of the Sekhem Flame within. Send out from your eye, arrows of fire to dispel all illness and discomfort. Just as you dispersed the enemies of Ra, so shall you scatter and destroy the illness within your children here."

A priestess adds the Sekhemet incense to the thurible along with a pinch of black cat hair.

High Priestess: "I bring breath to these who are the children of Ra, AU ERTU NIFA EN ENEN UNNU RA!"

The blue flame is now dispersed back into the earth by reversing it back through each person then down into the floor of the temple. Those who would place their petitions in the thurible are asked to come forward at this time. When each of the petitions has turned to ash, the ritual is closed.

High Priestess: "Sekhemet, The Powerful, we are grateful for your aid, Return now to your realm in the Seket-Hetep."

ANKUS, UTA, SENB"

All say: "Ankus, Uta, Senb!"

A libation of pomegranate juice is shared as the symbolic blood of Sekhemet. We all take a little time for private communion with the goddess before leaving. As we leave the darkened chamber of the small temple, we are met by vivid sunlight, the blazing Eye of Ra/Sekhemet herself.

Meditation of the Blue flame

The meditation of the Blue Flame is a healing method used by the temple priests and priestesses to put their patients in touch with their own life-force, the Sekhem Flame. The ancient Egyptians believed that the Sekhem existed in all living beings as the force that animated them. They also believed that during illness the Sekehem was weakened much like the concept of the Chi in

Chinese medicine. Ancient Egyptian healing was a holistic approach in which the physical, emotional and spiritual forces were all interconnected. Illness of the body started in the mind, the intellectual/spiritual realm. By the time that an illness had manifested physically, the Egyptian healer would have to go back to the source through meditation and Dream Therapy. The patient would be taught how to call upon their own Sekhem energy, how to move it through their body and how to heal themselves. Medicinal herbs and Aromatherapy were prescribed to heal the physical body, the Sekhem energy was called upon to heal the mind and the emotions.

Ritual Checklist:
    1 blue candle
    Natron
    Myrrh incense
    Almond oil

The first step in this meditation, as with all works of magic, begins with the purification of yourself and your working space. This is especially important when you are ready to call forth your own healing flame.

Begin by making sure that you will not be interrupted, that goes for ringing phones, doorbells etc. Then take a purifying bath in Natron water, (11/4 cup of salt to three tablespoons of bicarbonate of soda). When you are finished with your purification, dress in a loose fitting robe. Light your blue candle and some of the myrrh incense. Anoint yourself with the almond oil then lie flat on a bed or the floor.

With your arms out to the side take three deep Sekhem breaths. Visualize yourself at the steps of a magnificent temple-the temple of you.

In your minds eye see yourself walk up the steps and into the deep, dark interior of the temple. You walk through the courtyard, the Great Hall, the inner hall and finally, the Sanctuary. Inside the darkened interior of the Sanctuary, you can see a stone altar. On top of the stone altar is a shallow brazier in which a blue flame burns brightly. Come closer to that flame. Breathe it in so that it fills your body.

Allow the blue flame to burn away all illness and discomfort, filling any dark areas with radiant light. The blue flame is now energizing and healing your body. After a few minutes of circulating the blue flame inside your body, allow it to go back to its source in the center of the brazier. As you do so, keep for yourself what you need to heal yourself, transform yourself, and energize yourself. When you are finished, visualize yourself walking back out of the temple. Take three deep Sekhem breaths, relax and rise when you are ready.

Reversed Flame Spell

At any time you feel negativity around you, the Reversed Flame spell will send those bad vibes right back to their source. Much like a Reflect and Return ritual, the fire of Sekhemet will leave all judgment to the Gods. You just need to send it on its way!

Ritual Checklist:
> 1 red candle
> Hathor mirror
> Dragons Blood oil
> Frankincense
> Parchment or Papyrus
> Black ink
> Ritual time: Saturday of the waning moon, 9:00 pm

To prepare for your spell, you must first write in black ink, on a small square of either parchment or papyrus, those things that are affecting you in a negative way. They can be such things as gossip at work, conflicts with friends or family, or even a specific person.

Don't worry; you will not be harming anyone, just reflecting their own behavior back to them!

When that is done, inscribe the same thing on the red candle then anoint it with the Dragons Blood oil, and place it in front of your Hathor mirror.

Light the frankincense in your thurible then light the candle. As you do so, say these words:

Back! O' back! thou enemies of light,
Bringers of chaos you shall scatter before the piercing darts of Sekhemet's flame.

Visualize all your conflicts going back to their source; as they are reflected by the mirror into the Duat/Underworld and back to its place of origin.

Now place the parchment or papyrus into the thurible and let it burn to ash. Let the red candle burn all the way down. Dispose of the wax residue and the ashes by burying them in the ground.

Nefrem Eye Protection Charm

There were many magical stones in ancient Egypt; most of them are semi-precious such as turquoise, malachite, and lapis lazuli. However the stone that was most associated with lion power and the strength of Sekhemet was Tigers Eye. This mysterious stone blazed like the tawny eyes of the lioness herself and was often carved into Sekhemet and Bastet amulets.

Ritual Checklist:
Tigers Eye stone
Small red felt bag
A pinch of golden cat fur
Catnip herb
Cat claw leavings (from shedding)
1 small piece of snake skin

Lotus oil
Sekhemet incense
A statue or picture of Sekhemet
1 red candle
Ritual time: The full moon, 9:00pm

On the night of the full moon, prepare for your ritual by taking a purification bath using Natron and five drops of the lotus oil.

When the moon is high in the sky at approximately 9:00 pm, light your red candle. Take three deep Sekhem breaths. With your arms raised in the Ka position invoke the goddess Sekhemet.

"Sekhemet Per Aha, Lady of Great Magic,
whose Flaming Eye drove back the enemies of Ra,
I invoke thee and ask your aid in this work of magic.
Just as you poised vigilant on the brow of the God,
so shall you protect and defend all that would seek to
dissemble and destroy the Right and True."

After your invocation, light the incense. One-by-one, pass the ingredients for your charm through the incense smoke. Then starting with the catnip herb, place them into the small red bag. When you are finished, 'show them to the flame' by holding the bag up to the candle and visualizing the power of the flame entering the bag. Place the bag at the base of your statue or picture of Sekhemet and let the candle burn all the way down.

Amulet of the Papyrus Scepter

The amulet of the papyrus scepter was used for the living and the deceased to promote health, vigor and the renewal of youth. It was most often made of a stone called 'Mother of Emerald' or green or blue faience. They were placed in a row around the neck of the mummy; they could also be worn or carried by

the living. The papyrus scepter took on new meaning in the 26th dynasty when it came to represent the power of the goddesses Sekhemet, Isis and the serpent goddess Renenet of Abundant harvests. It was said to be placed in the hands of the deceased by Tehuti himself, to serve as a sort of 'Staff of Life' for the Afterlife.

Ritual Checklist:

Blue or green fimo clay
Red cord or thread
Pomegranate seeds
Myrrh incense
Ankh
1 white candle and one gold candle
Ritual time: Full moon, 9:00 pm

On the night of the full moon begin creating your amulet with the clay. It should be oval in shape and approximately 11/2 inches long. Put it in the oven for the prescribed time. While it is baking, light your incense and candles. Then pass your Ankh through the incense smoke three times to cleanse it. When your amulet is done, place it between the two candles. Sprinkle the pomegranate seeds around your amulet and at the base of both candles. As you do so, say these words:

"It is in a sound state, and I am in a sound state,
It is not injured, and I am not injured,
It is not worn away and I am not worn away."

When that is done, take up your Ankh and hold it by the loop end. Raise your left palm so that moonlight can strike it. Feel the energy circulate through you, then point your Ankh towards your amulet and take three deep Sekhem breaths, now say:

"The left and right eye of Ra are joined in me, the moon and the sun, The Fire of the Lady of Flame, Sekhemet brings Life, Health, Strength, Ankus Uta Senb!"

When you are done, let the candles burn all the way down. Leave your amulet in the moonlight overnight. The next morning you can attach the red cord to it and it is ready to be worn around your neck.

The Ritual of the Mehenet Eye
A Sekhemet Healing ritual

The healing power of Sekhemet is most often associated with her ability to "burn or scorch out" illness, and eradicate it with her purifying flames. This ritual calls for creating her 'Golden Eye' the destroyer of all enemies. In ancient times the 'Eye' was made of mirror, glass or even crystal. In these times though there are many more ready materials such as a piece of concave glass or a magnifying lens.

Ritual Checklist:
1 piece of parchment or papyrus
Dragons Blood ink
Dried Lemon leaves
Thurible
Beeswax sheets, natural or white in color
1 piece of red cloth either cotton or silk
Pomegranate juice
Natron water
Bread and red wine or grape juice
Myrrh nuggets
Ritual Time: Noon, 12:00

Before the sun climbs to its zenith, create your wax figurine. Mold the beeswax in your hands until it is soft, then, shape it into a form resembling yourself or someone who has requested healing. Add to the wax any personal effects that you may have such as hair and fingernails. Leave a cavity in the wax doll wherever that illness is located, such as: the heart region for healing of the physical and emotional heart. Set the doll aside.

Next create your Mehenet Eye by obtaining a piece of concave glass or a lens from a magnifying glass. When you have found something suitable, cleanse it in the Natron water and set it aside.

In your thurible, place the myrrh nuggets on the bottom and the dried lemon leaves on top. On top of that put the piece of parchment. On the piece of parchment you will have written in the Dragons Blood ink, all those illnesses that you would have destroyed. Then raise your Mehenet Eye to the sun and say these words:

"Thou flaming eye of the serpent Mehenet, I invoke thee from the dark regions of the Duat, come forth and release the darts of fire that would heal_____(person's name). Destroy all disease and illness, be the breath of Sekhemet!"

Angle your 'eye' so that the rays of the sun are magnified by it, shining it directly into your thurible until the parchment catches fire. Breathe the Sekhem breath on it gently. Visualize all illness being burned away. When the offerings have burnt to ashes, it is time to release Mehenet:

"Back O' back serpent of Sekhemet-Ra,
Return to the dark regions of the Duat where you will remain ever vigilant."

When it has burned down to ashes, mix in nine drops of pomegranate juice to form a paste. Put the paste into the cavity of your wax figurine and seal it with the candle wax. Wrap the cloth around it, and bury the figurine where the ill person must pass by daily such as near their front door.

CHAPTER NINE

Bastet and the temple of Tel Basta

"I have come from the House of the Leonine One,
I left there for the House of Isis,
I saw her hidden mysteries in that she let me see the birth of
the Great God."

Ancient Egyptian coffin text

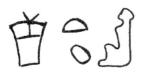

The Radiant Eye of the Moon

If Sekhemet is the personification of the blazing eye of the sun, Bastet the Cat Goddess is her twin flame, the radiant eye of the moon. While Sekhemet represented the destructive, purgative qualities of Ra, Bastet represented the god's beneficial life-sustaining, solar qualities.

In fact it could be said that a myriad of mysteries that comprise Egypt are rolled up in one complex, multi-faceted form, Bastet, the feline goddess supreme.

The first evidence of her worship appeared in Egyptian history in the 2nd dynasty of the Archaic Period approximately 3200 B.C. Here in the city of Heliopolis, the Temple of the Sun, in Lower Egypt, she appeared in lioness form as a solar deity and was referred to as the 'Little Cat' while Sekhemet was named the 'Big Cat'. As a daughter of Ra she fought back the enemies of the sun, in the form of the serpent of darkness, Apep. This battle, which was fought during the hours of darkness, when all cats are most active, awarded her the title of 'Shetat' the Hidden One. In Memphis during the Old Kingdom, her role as a Solar Deity took another form associated with the Memphis Triad as Sekhemet-

Bast-Ra. Here, she worked together with her sister Sekhemet to vanquish the enemies of light. In one version of myth, Ra gives her control over the Serpent of Wisdom, the Ureaus, as a reward for vanquishing the Serpent of Darkness, Apep. This association led to much confusion concerning her appearance at the time.

Both Bastet and Sekhemet were represented as lion headed goddesses. What distinguished Bastet, called the 'Lady of Ankh-Taui' from her fierce counterpart, was her headdress and robes. Sekhemet was clothed in red with the solar disk surrounded by the Ureaus serpent. Bastet appeared in green robes with a crown of multiple serpents encircling her head and carrying a Sistrum in her hands.

Other solar associations of Bastet were that of a Great Nourisher, where her gentle fructifying lunar rays promoted the fertility of the fields. Cat effigies and votive offerings were often placed in the fields for just this purpose. The ancient Egyptians also believed that a cat's eyes could map the Sun's journey across the sky by watching the size of their pupils in relation to the horizon. A phenomenon that was proved true in the 20th century by Roger Carras the author of 'A Cat is Waiting' in which he observed that cats possessed an internal, global positioning system that allowed them to scan the horizon for the Sun's angle.

So strong were Bastet's solar associations that in ancient Egypt, at the time of a solar eclipse, people gathered outside of their houses in the streets shaking Sistrums to cheer Bastet in her triumph over the evil Apep, the Serpent of Darkness.

By the Middle Kingdom, Bastet was almost always seen in cat form. A circumstance, which in part could be associated with the migrations of lions out of Egypt as well as popularity of domestic cats at the time. She was seen as a slender, long eared cat sometimes wearing a pectoral collar with the Sacred Eye in the center, pierced ears and a scarab on her head. The tufts of hair in her ears resembled the feathers of Maat the goddess of the Right and True. The scarab represented her powers of fertility and rebirth and the Sacred Eye, the eye that was entrusted to her by her twin brother Horus. In her form as a woman she was depicted regally robed, holding her symbols of the Sistrum, Aegis and Basket in her arms.

The Sistrum is the symbol of love and joy, a reflection of Bastet's association with the Goddess of Love, Hathor. The Aegis is a curious symbol, the only one known in Egyptian mythology. It is a small crescent shaped shield with a lion's head in the center. The basket, which was often shown on one arm, contained a litter of kittens nestled in it, a symbol of fertility and familial devotion.

The Soul of Isis

By far the most important association for the goddess Bastet was that of the Soul of Isis. Her very name Bastet was thought to be derived from Ba the word for soul and Auset the name of Isis.

In her principle temple of Bubastis or Tel Basta she was known as the Daughter of Isis and Osiris. Isis and Osiris as well as Bastet's son Khonsu were all lunar deities. In this guise, she embodied the mystery and magic of the moon. Great healing powers were attributed to her as the Moon-Eye of Ra, powers that were channeled through her Divine Mother Isis.

Like Isis, Bastet was a favorite and approachable goddess to the common people. Statues and amulets of her could be found in every Egyptian home from the royalty to the peasantry. She represented familial love, fertility and the protection of children. She was even thought to have a special influence over pregnant women and appeared as one of the goddesses of the birth chamber. Her son Khonsu, was said to make women fruitful and to make the human germ grow in the mothers womb. Phallic symbols from the 18th dynasty were depicted as a penis with a cat head, that of the 'Tom' cat Khonsu.

When couples decided to wed in ancient Egypt, they would go first to the votive stalls and purchase an amulet of Bastet and her kittens. Choosing one that depicted the number of children they wished to have. They would then either wear the amulet or hang it above their bed as a fertility charm.

Bastet was also a goddess of pleasure and sensuality. Her great yearly festival at Bubastis was according to Herodotus the Greek historian "Ecstatic, and full of affectionate zeal.".

As 'The Lady of Music and Dance' Bastet was the patron goddess of musicians and dancers, who in ancient Egypt were primarily women. This was a natural association, since cats were thought to possess their own special musical instrument, which produced purring and trilling sounds, coupled with the natural suppleness of their bodies.

As Shetat, the Hidden One, Bastet was also a goddess of the Underworld. With the feline capabilities of seeing in the dark, she would protect the soul of the deceased by taking part in the funerary rites in a protection ritual called 'The Cat of Lapis Lazuli'.

Magic wands made of the curved ivory of Hippopotami tusks were buried with the deceased. They were cat headed, and were inscribed with the horoscope of the deceased person.

The Nine Lives of Ra

The popular belief that cats possessed nine lives began in Egypt. The Egyptian calendar was a lunar one, consisting of nine months. These nine months comprised the nine spheres of the Egyptian astrological calendar. Ra was reborn each lunar month from the womb of the sky goddess Nut. The number nine was also an important magical number for the Egyptians, composed of three trinities, three being an active number and one that also represented the pyramid.

Bastet alone, as both a lunar and a solar deity, could traverse freely through both worlds. The worlds of the conscious and the unconscious, the physical and the spiritual, absorbing and reflecting the powers of both.

Magical Attributes:

Name: Bastet, Bast, Pasht, Shetat, The Hidden One, and The
Lady of the East

Symbol: Cat, Aegis, Basket with kittens, Sistrum

Planet: Venus

Color: Turquoise green

Metal: Yellow gold

Number: 9

Tools: The Sistrum

Herbs: Catnip

Key words: Patroness of song and dance, Love, Joy, Romance
and passion, fertility, childbirth and familial love.

Tel-Basta, City of the Cat Cult

The city of Tel Basta, called Bubastis in ancient times, is located in
the eastern Delta Region of Lower Egypt. It was the capitol of the
seventh Nome, Am-Khent, the Nome reputed to have the thigh of
the god Osiris buried in it. It was also the premier center of the
Cult of the Cat Goddess Bastet and her sons Mihos and
Horhekenu.

Built entirely of red granite, the temple stood like an island in
the center of the town. It was built around an ancient Persea tree,
the symbolic tree in which Bastet battled the serpent Apep;
surrounded by the waters of the Nile and could only by

approached by ferry. The exact age of the original temple is unknown; but stone stele found from the Old Kingdom, carrying inscriptions from the pharaohs Khafre and Khufu, have been found dating from the 4th dynasty. The remains of a Ka temple built for the Pharaoh Pepi I of the 6th dynasty were found as well, with an inscription identifying Pepi as having the 'Heart of Bastet'.

Over the hundreds of years, the temple of Bubastis, like all the temples, went through many changes, falling into disrepair many times. It was finally rebuilt in the age of Taurus, by the great builder- Pharaoh himself Rameses II of the 18th dynasty. It was during this period also that the mummification of cats became more popular, so much so that hundreds of feline mummies were buried along the course of the Nile as well as in the cemetery of Bubastis.

Tel Basta/Bubastis did not reach its height of glory though, until the 22nd dynasty when it became the capital of Egypt. Bastet then took precedence over all the other goddesses. During which time King Osorkon built a magnificent festival hall in her honor. A relief on the walls of his chapel showed the king offering Bastet the amulet of the 'Sacred Eye' the (Wejat or Uchat) eye, stating these words; "I give thee every land in obeisance, I give thee all power like Ra".

The city of Bubastis was also the center of one of the greatest festivals of the ancient world, the 'Festival of Bast' which took place in April and May. A celebration of love, romance and fertility, this great festival drew revelers from all over Egypt and the ancient world swelling to proportions in the hundreds of thousands.

The best account of the festival comes from ancient writings of the Greek historian Herodotus. He wrote of a merry festival attended by people from all walks of life. Bejeweled nobles cruising up the Nile in their elaborately decorated boats were greeted by the people on shore with a great show of music and singing. Men, women and children crowded into the ferries that would bring them to the temple so that they might lay their sacrifices and offerings before the goddess Bastet. Wine and beer flowed freely, all manner of instruments were played; Sistrums, tambours, harps and flutes. There was dancing in the street, and women would playfully lift their skirts to lure new lovers in the spirit of spring passion.

Tel Basta March 20th, 2000

Ever since my first trip to Egypt I have wanted to visit the temple of The Cat Goddess Bastet. Ten years ago, it was not possible because the temple was not yet open to the public. Recent excavations, however, have finally made it feasible. Located as it is on the road to Alexandria, the trip to Tel Basta involved a long bus ride through the center of many bustling towns of the Delta region. Tel Basta itself was located in the center of one of these towns, the modern city of Zagazig.

Destroyed by an earthquake in ancient times, the first impression of the temple is deflating in its ruinous state. All that is still standing are a few pillars and columns tossed about like giant building blocks. When we took a closer look though, those pillars and broken statuary radiated a special energy of their own. The carvings were unusual and magical, depicting scenes of priestesses performing rituals, musicians, and dancers performing at the great festival of Bast.

Though small and in a state of ruin, the temple has much to offer still. In the center of the temple grounds, among the tumbled down stone monuments is a sacred well. A well that is visited even today, from women who travel from all over to partake of the waters. Waters purported to bring fertility to barren women.

Lastly, and by far the most mysterious part of Tel Basta, is the Cat Cemetery. A place where row upon row of oval shaped graves held the mummies of hundreds of sacred cats. It is here among

these tombs and the Ba souls of divine felines that we have chosen
to do our ritual.

Dedication to Bastet

The purpose of our ritual today will be to reconnect with the
goddess Bastet to bring some of her divine qualities into our lives
and those of our loved ones. It is designed also to be a ritual of
dedication for our own feline companions. Many of us have
brought photos of our own cats to place upon the altar, as well as
any Bastet statuary that is to be blessed.

Ritual Checklist:

Parchment paper
Sistrum
Photos of cat companions
Statue of Bastet
Bast incense
Ritual wine
Bread
Small scarab
Milk
1 sheet of gold beeswax
Temple Dancer

Our guide, the intrepid Amr, has chosen the perfect spot for our ritual, a private clearing in the middle of the cemetery. Our altar is to be the rim of one of the cat tombs, on it we have spread a white altar cloth and set it up with statuary of Bastet, Sistrums and photographs of our cat companions and loved ones. The incense is lit and, one by one we line up for the Sistrum purification, the first step in our ritual. When that is done we all turn to face the East to greet the goddess.

High Priestess:

"Bastet Per Aha, I invoke thee, thou that hast risen from the soul of Isis,

Come forth as Bastet the Lady of the East, Eye of the Moon, Shetat,

Come forth playing your tambour, gentle and fierce protectress of the

Children of man."

All Say: (shaking their Sistrums five times)

"Hika,

Hika,

Hika,

Hika,

Hika."

High Priestess: "Those who would come forth and petition the Lady do so now."

The participants come forward to the altar bringing with them the pieces of parchment on which they have written the name of a family member who is in need of healing. I gather them up and place them in the center of the gold sheet of wax along with the scarab and some of the Bastet incense. When that is done the wax is formed into a ball and placed on the altar.

High Priestess: "This Utchat eye, shall be as a reflection of the Eye of Almighty Ra, I ask that Bastet look upon these petitions and place upon them Ankus Uta Senb, Life, Health, Strength, and deliver all illness and discomfort back into the Abyss from which it came."

The symbolic 'Eye' is set upon the altar and all the participants are asked to join hands. The temple dancer begins her dance to raise the Sekhem energy. I ask everyone to close their eyes and envision the gentle healing rays of the sun entering their bodies, illuminating, them and filling them with energy and joy. This energy is then passed through the hands of the High Priestess, Yours Truly, to the photographs of our feline companions. One, by one, I hold up the photos charging them with the task of magical companion.

High Priestess: "In the name of the goddess Bastet, keeper of the Utchat Eye, I charge_____(name of cat) to serve as protector, healer and magical companion to _____(name of participant). To walk in this world and the Duat, to be ever vigilant in the service of the Mother, Bastet."

The Sistrums are shaken five times after each name to send the charges out in to the universe. After all the feline companions have been given their charge, the Sekhem energy is grounded with everyone taking what they need for themselves and allowing the rest to go back to its source.

High Priestess: "We thank you Lady, and present you with these offerings."

The bread, wine, and milk are presented one by one to the east. The milk is poured into the mud brick tomb along with a piece of bread. The symbolic Eye, is placed in there as well and the libation of wine and bread is shared by all the participants.

Bastet Child Blessing

One of Bastet's most important duties as a goddess of the family was to bless and protect children. Just as a mother cat is fiercely protective of her kittens, so did the Egyptians associate this protectiveness with their own children. Every household, either grand or humble, had a special niche for Bastet as protectress of the home and children. Bastet was invoked at the birth of a child and she was called upon thereafter to protect them from illness and injury. This Bastet Baby Blessing has very ancient origins and must take place nine days after the birth of a child.

On the night of the eighth day the parents and the godparents must light a white candle. Underneath the candle on a piece of papyrus or parchment must be written a magical name for the child, this name having come to the parents and godparents through meditation. On the ninth day the candle that has stayed lit the longest, will be the one to determine the magical name of the child. This magical name will be the name the child will use in ritual. A power name, it will act as a personal totem for the child throughout his or her life.

Ritual Checklist:

Statue or picture of Bastet
Lettuce oil or Olive oil
1 blue cloth approximately 2 feet square
Sistrum
Ankh
Cat amulet or cat figurine necklace
Lettuce seeds
Milk
Lotus Oil
Bastet Incense
Small white robe for baby
Ritual time: Noon

When the sun is high in the sky, prepare your ritual space by first purifying it with Natron water, then follow that with a consecration using the Bastet incense. Set up your altar with the statue of Bastet, Sistrum, Ankh, ritual oil and white candles or an oil lamp. If at all possible, your ritual oil should be lettuce oil, an oil sacred to Min the fertility God. If that is not possible you can substitute it with olive oil. Everyone attending the Blessing must be purified as well through a purifying bath and then dressed in pure white garments. The baby to be blessed must wear a white robe or christening gown. The blessing is to be attended by the family and the godparents, along with special friends. Before entering the ritual space each person must have the Sistrum Purification by one of the priestesses. The child, its parents and the godparents are then led forward to stand before the altar.

High Priestess: "Bastet, Per Aha, I invoke thy presence here today to bless this child, a living God/Goddess, Neter, a shining being so that he/she shall have a new name and blessing according to the laws Maati, the Right and True."

Priestess: "Have you chosen the Hikau name for this child?"

Parent: "Yes we have."

The parents now hand to a priestess the name on the parchment paper. She passes it to the High Priestess.

High Priestess: "This sacred name shall be known only to those who are present here and the priest and priestess of the temple. It shall from this day forth be the 'Hikau' of this child, the name of his/her Ren that shall be known on earth and in the land of Amenti."

All say:
"Hika,
Hika,
Hika,
Hika,
Hika."

High Priestess: "Come forth O' sons of Horus!"

At this time four family members are asked to come forth to represent the four sons of Horus and their respective goddesses. The priestess hands them the blue cloth. Each person grasps a corner of the fabric. The child is then placed in the center of the cloth, the symbolic lotus flower.

The High Priestess then anoints the child starting with the forehead, the heart region, the sex organs and the legs.

High Priestess:

"May the Tatta, (head) be clear,

May the Ab, (heart) be pure,

May the Xerui (male) Hem (female) be controlled,

May the Menti (legs, representing physical body) be as strong as the

pillars of the temple to support the holy vessel of this child, Ankus,

Uta, Senb!"

The High Priestess then raises her hands in the Ka position allowing the power of Ra to enter her body. She then places the Ankh to the child's lips.

High Priestess: "Receive now this breath of life, the divine Sekhem and with it, your new name and blessing. In the name of Bastet, Soul of Isis, Lady of the East I give you this new name. I give you the name of _____ (name that has been chosen previously) and with it the blessings of _____ (special gifts that will be channeled through the priestess for the child at the time of the blessing). This is the name you shall be known as in the presence of all the gods in the halls of the double Maati."

The four sons of Horus present the child, who is still lying in the center of the lotus, first to the east then to the west, north and south.

East: "Hail to thee that ruleth the east, Lord Duamutef, jackal headed son of Horus, Neith Warrior goddess and protectress I present to thee _____(magical name of child)."

West: "Hail to thee that ruleth the west, Lord Quebsenuf, falcon headed son of Horus, Selkit Scorpion goddess of magic, I present to thee _____(magical name of child)."

North: "Hail to thee that ruleth the north, Lord Hapi, ape headed son of Horus, Nepthys, Goddess of the underworld I present to thee _____(magical name of child)."

South: "Hail to thee that ruleth the south, Lord Imsety, human headed son of Horus, Sekhemet lioness of the desert who guards the eternal flame, I present to thee _____ (magical name of child)."

When the child has been presented to all the elements he/she is brought once more to the altar. The parents and the godparents stand before the High Priestess. The parents carry a small dish containing the lettuce seeds and the godparents carrying a bowl of milk.

High Priestess: "From this day forth the parents and godparents of this child shall keep a shrine to the Lady Bastet so that she will protect and nurture this child. They must also present an offering this day in her honor."

The seeds and the milk are placed next to the goddess on the altar to represent rebirth and nourishment in the child's life. The cat amulet is also placed around the child's neck at this time.

High Priestess: "O' Bastet, we thank you for your presence here today and the presence of all the Neters, we thank you for the blessings that you have bestowed upon this child,

Hika,

Hika,

Hika,

Hika,

Hika."

The priestess and all present shake their Sistrums to send out the words of power. The child is bundled in the blue cloth and the wine and bread is shared.

Sistrum Purification Ritual

The Sistrum purification ritual is always the first thing that is done before any Egyptian ceremony or ritual. This special cleansing uses the power of sound, and sound vibrations to dispel any negative energies that you might be holding onto to. After the negative energies have been driven out, the Sistrum acts like a tuning fork to attune you with the macrocosmic energy. Just another way that the ancient Egyptians used the power of sound!

To begin your Sistrum purification ritual you must first start at the persons head. Shake your Sistrum five times in a circular pattern as you do say these words:

(Insert Photo #34 here)
"Isis Per Aha, I invoke thee, may your mind be clear! Hika, hika, hika, hika, hika!"

Then shake your Sistrum five times at the heart center in a circular pattern as you do so, say these words:

"Isis Per Aha, I invoke thee, may your heart be pure! Hika, hika ,hika ,hika, hika!"

Finally shake your Sistrum five times in a circular pattern at the junction of the person's legs as you do so, say these words:
"Isis Per Aha, I invoke thee, may your body be strong! Hika, hika, hika, hika, hika!"

The Sistrum purification is now complete, and the temple can be entered. Sistrum purification can also be used in healing rituals to cleanse or rid the body, mind and soul of discomfort and disease.

Bastet Fire of Love Spell

The sensuous and procreative nature of cats was recognized and celebrated by the Egyptians. The Festival of Bast was a prime example, the theme of the celebration was fun loving and ecstatic; Women displayed their charms and allure in hopes of seduction and men danced and drank wine in abandon. Both men and women exchanged playful, sexual innuendoes and jokes. The act of love in ancient Egypt was referred to as joyous and natural and was called 'Spending a Merry Day'.

Bastet, like Hathor, was a goddess of sexual mystery. When it came to love magic, people appealed to her to provoke lust and attraction in a potential mate. The following spell is designed to incite the 'Fire of Love' to provide lustful opportunity and to leave the rest up to the Gods!

Ritual Checklist:

Musk oil

Patchouli leaves

7 pieces of red thread

7 red candles

Black cat hair

1 large red rose petal

1 sheet of red beeswax

Ritual time: waxing moon, 9:00pm

Begin your spell in the waxing period, seven days before the full moon. When the moon is high in the sky, mold your beeswax into the likeness of your lover, making sure to exaggerate the genital areas.

On one candle carve the name of Bast-Sekhemet. Anoint the candle with the musk oil. Using your fingernail, trace the initial of your intended on the red rose petal. Then create a cavity in the chest of your wax figurine, and place the red rose petal inside of it. Light the Bast-Sekhemet candle. As you do so, say these words:

"The Fire of Bast-Sekhemet, shall flame the desire of _____(lover's name), may she/he be consumed with desire for me."

Then place some of the patchouli leaves inside the wax figurine, saying:

"May _____ (lover's name) be filled with the strength of my desire."

Sprinkle some of the black cat hair into the cavity next, saying these words:

"The power of Bastet, is in the heart of _____(lover's name)!"

Close the cavity. Then starting at the head, wind the red threads one by one around it. Seal the threads with some drippings from your candle. When that is done anoint the figurine with the musk oil. As you do so, say these words:

"O' Bastet you have secured the passion of _____(lover's name) with the ribbons of the Seven Hathors, by the light of this month's full moon we shall become as one!"

When you are done, let the candle burn all the way down. The next night and every night for six more days, burn one red candle at the same time each night. Place the wax figurine next to the candle each night. On the night of the full moon when you burn your last candle bury the wax along with the figurine in a place where your intended lover is sure to pass.

Bastet Protection Spell

As a protectress of the home, Bastet's power extended to all the family members including the family animals, as if she was fiercely protecting her own kittens. This protection spell involves the creation of a special type of altar to Bastet, one that can be worked with on an ongoing basis.

Ritual Checklist:
1 small basket
Pieces of parchment paper
Lotus oil
Red thread
Vervain herb
1 large Tiger Eye stone
Cat hair
Cat claws (shedded ones)

Small cat figurines, one for each family member (they can also be pictures of cats)

On the night of the full moon place your basket outside so that it can absorb the lunar energy. Write the name of each family member including pets on individual pieces of parchment. Tie them with the red string and set aside. The next night, retrieve your basket. Place the vervain herb at the bottom along with the cat hair and nails. Anoint the parchment scrolls and the figurines then place them in the basket as well. As you do so, say these words:

"Bastet Per Aha, you shall bring Life, Health and Strength, ANKUS UTA SENB to this household! You shall protect all that dwell here from all that would cause evil or discomfort!"

Lastly, add the Tiger Eye stone, the Shetat Eye:

"The sacred eye of Shetat, the Hidden One, shall see through all false words and deeds, find and recover any stolen possessions, protect this family, with the mighty fire of Ra himself."

When the basket is complete, set it in a place where it will not be disturbed. On each full moon replace the herbs and cat hair. Set out an offering to Bastet in the form of a small bowl of milk next to her picture or statue. You can add family members to the basket each full moon if necessary, always remembering to thank the goddess in return!

Bastet Ritual wine

Bastet was sometimes known as 'The Lady of Wine', because her festivals were so Bacchanalian in style, with drunkenness an accepted way to gain spiritual ecstasy. Some of the most famous of the white wines of ancient Egypt came out of the Delta region of Bubastis. This particular recipe for ritual wine contains magical herbs and can be prepared ahead of time for your rituals.

Recipe:

1 bottle of white wine, preferably a Muscat or comparable vintage
2 cups of raw unfiltered honey
Vervain herb
Dried rose petals
1 pinch of ginger
1 tsp of cinnamon

In a large jar, steep the herbs in the wine. Allow your wine to steep out of direct sunlight for one week. At the end of that week, add the honey. Refrigerate it over night and your delicious Bastet wine will be ready for your next ritual.

CHAPTER TEN

Tehuti and the Great Pyramid of Giza

"Woe unto those who wait, for they must return again, unconscious and unknowing to the seed ground of the stars, where they await a new beginning"
Tehuti

The Divine Scribe

The origins of the God Tehuti whom the Greeks referred to as Thoth/Hermes come to us steeped in as much mystery as the pyramids themselves. Tehuti was known as the first high priest of Egypt, a foreigner from the land of the west that was said to be a self-begotten and self-conceived one.

Egyptian myth depicts him as the oldest brother of the goddess Isis, and the son of Atum Ra the Sun God. Other versions of the myth however which are documented in the in the 'Pyramid Texts' state his origins as the son of Nun, making him the brother of Ra, and therefore connecting him with the Solar realm and possibly another solar system as well. Other associations have named him the 'Heart of Ra' the spokesman and channel for the Creator God Ra. He was credited with uttering the word or sound that hatched the egg of creation from the sacred Ibis bird, which in turn gave birth to all living creatures.

Magical properties were attributed to his voice, including a sonic quality that was reputed to be able to manipulate matter. He was the speaker of the 'Sacred Language' the 'Words of Power' and the 'Hekau' a language that was thought to have been brought with him from another more advanced civilization, and that later became the precursor of the Egyptian language itself.

From what advanced civilization did he come from? The only records we have come from an Egyptian priest named Manetho, a follower of the Thrice Divine Hermes, a priest of Hermopolis who lived during the Ptolomaic period. For many years of his life he painstakingly poured over ancient script to provide a history of this intriguing God. A history that was later related by such classic historians as Herodotus and Plato.

From his research he concluded that Tehuti arrived in Egypt during the constellation or Age of Cancer, 300 years before the floods and the destruction of Atlantis. He came as a missionary and colonist bringing with him the wisdom of a more advanced civilization. The knowledge of science, mathematics, astronomy, astrology, architecture, art and writing. In his role as Magi he presided over the religious development of Egypt teaching them the art of healing and magic.

As a Lord of Karma, he presided over the 'Weighing of the Heart' ceremony, recording the deeds of the deceased during their lifetime. The deceased's heart, representing the heart of their soul, would then be weighed against a feather. If their heart was lighter than the feather the deceased would live forever in the Elysian fields of the Afterlife, if their heart was heavier than the feather it would be devoured by a monster and the deceased would never to be reborn again.

As the Lord of Books, Tehuti was credited with being the author of the Funerary Texts that gave instruction for the deceased in the realm of the Afterlife.

Tehuti was also said to have been the inventor of the Solar Calendar, and was giving credit for adding five days to the calendar year from the original 360 to 365. In the myth, Tehuti challenged the god Ra to a game of draughts, upon winning he asked Ra to add the additional five days to the calendar.

This curious story has often been thought to give an explanation of the time when the earth shifted on its axis, therefore adding the additional five days to its circuit around the Sun.

Tehuti is often depicted as an Ibis headed god with a crescent moon headdress with writing materials in his hands. His other totem animal is the baboon, which is thought to be the representation of an alter ego or a curious shape-shifting disguise.

A patron god of writing and language, he counted among his followers; priests, scribes and magicians. He was the creator of the Akashic records also known as the Emerald Tablets, 35,000 books of knowledge that were given into the Egyptian priesthood.

What then became of these books of knowledge? Were they destroyed when the Egyptian priesthood was forced underground, or is there still tangible evidence of the advanced knowledge imparted by the God of Knowledge, Tehuti?

For this you must look to the magnificent monument that dominates the Giza plateau like a giant ray of sun come to earth from the heavens. For here lies the evidence of Tehuti's greatest work, the Great Pyramid.

Magical Attributes:

Name: Tehuti, Thoth, Hermes

Symbol: Ibis bird, Baboon

Color: Amethyst

Metal: Silver

Number: 1

Tools: Caduceus, Scribes Palette

Herbs: Musk, Storax

Key Words: "As it is above, so it shall be below." Earthly application of natural laws.

The Greatest Temple on Earth

What can be said about the Great Pyramid of Giza that hasn't been said before? Perhaps that this magnificent monument was not built as a tomb, as supposed by Egyptologists and Historians alike? That perhaps this mysterious architectural marvel, in which, no mummies or funerary evidence has ever found, had been built for another, more sacred purpose.

For thousands of years the Great pyramid and the pyramid complex has cast a spell on all that have beheld them. Explorers, scientists, mathematicians and philosophers from as far back as ancient times have speculated upon the exact purpose of the pyramids.

How and when they were built, is yet another mystery, one that has not been solved even to this day. It has been speculated that the Great pyramid was built by a pharaoh named Cheops that ruled during the 4th dynasty, in approximately 2644BC. Cheops was the son of Sneferu. Sneferu was credited with the building of the Step pyramid.

For the most part classical history has accepted this, and it was theorized after some red paint cartouches were found on the walls of the inner chambers of the pyramid. The cartouches were identified as belonging to the pharaoh Khufu, who was called Cheops by the Greeks. Even that evidence could not be entirely proven and many historians believe that the cartouches were of a much earlier king that was unknown to the Egyptians.

The actual date in which the pyramids were built remains as mystery as well. The Greek historian Herodotus reported in his 'Natural History' that the pyramids were built 300 years before the flood. Arab historians such as Ebn Wasuf Shah believe that they were much older and that according to some ancient inscriptions the Great pyramid was built when 'The Lyre was in the constellation of Cancer', which would be approximately 73,000 years ago. Also, that the pyramids were built to contain books of sacred science and that in the advent of the Great Flood, the books would be protected so that the knowledge would not be lost.

Who knows? The inscriptions to support such a theory may

well have been in the possession of the Arab invaders. Were they not the ones that stripped the Great Pyramid of its casing stones to build their Mosques? Those same stones that were said to be covered with many strange and unusual symbols?

Many years later, in the 20th century, information was discovered that further confused the issue. It was discovered by a computer recreation of the stars and constellations, that the pyramids were perfectly aligned with the constellation of Orion. For that alignment to be accurate, the pyramids would have to had been built in at least 10,000 BC, the approximate time of the flooding of the Nile.

Contradictions aside, when comparing the Great pyramid with all the rest of the monuments in Egypt one thing becomes startlingly clear; these monuments are unlike any to be found in the land.

Yes, it is true that there are many pyramids in Egypt, over 80 that are known of today. These pyramids were built during the Pyramid Age, in the 4th and 5th dynasties and were for the most part built as mortuary temples. None of them, however, compare with the mathematical and esoteric perfection of the Great Pyramid.

Could it be that the Great pyramid was the original model for the rest of the pyramids? Could it also be as supposed that they were built by the first settlers of an advanced race, the Master Race, that appeared in the Nile valley after the destruction of Atlantis?

Archeologists have garnered no evidence to support this theory. The practitioners of Egyptian Magic and the Isian Tradition believe it to be true, for that story has been passed down to us through our teachings. Therefore, for us, it is the spiritual significance of these monuments that we are concerned with.

Temples of Initiation

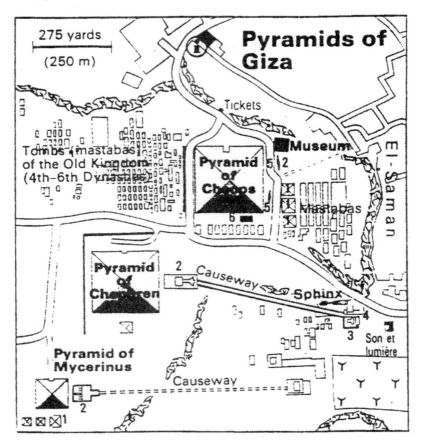

"Whereas externally, the pyramid symbolized the creative principle of Nature, and illustrated also the principles of mathematics, astronomy and astrology, within the building itself was the site of initiation. A temple of initiation where men rose towards the Gods and the Gods descended towards man."
Madame Blavatsky, Isis Unveiled

Again, we must thank that fearless, Greek historian Herodotus for leaning from the priests a glimpse into the archaic history of pt. For he confirmed what the practitioners of Egyptian Magic have always known, that settlers from an advanced civilization such as Atlantis came to Nile valley in predynastic Egypt. That they brought with them, a complete system of writing, astrology, astronomy and mathematics including the sacred geometry. That they were led by the first high priest of Egypt Tehuti, also known as Thoth to the Greeks.

Tehuti was the leader of a small group of people that emigrated from the land of the West after the destruction of Atlantis. He came to Egypt to build the greatest temple on earth, the Great pyramid. These monuments were created as living symbols of the interconnection between humankind and the universe. In Tehuti's own words, familiar words, that have survived even now in the magical philosophies of today; 'As it is above, so it shall be below'. The pyramid served as a link and a conduit in which the enlightened soul strove to reach ultimate perfection on the earthly plane, therefore being able to transcend to the heavens in which he came.

Through the teachings of Tehuti, the Divine Scribe, the pyramid is seen as a cornerstone of the Egyptian Mysteries. By its very shape it embodies several universal truths. Its base set upon red granite of which the depth has never been found symbolizes the fire element, the element of manifestation. The four corners of the pyramid are perfectly aligned within a hairs breadth with the cardinal points of the compass; East, South, West and North. The very top or point represents the Sekhem or Spirit-Life force much like the symbology of the pentagram. The pyramid when unfolded not only reveals the elemental associations on each side but the related signs of the zodiac as well that represent the stages the human spirit evolves through to reach ultimate perfection.

Each one of the four sides also represents respectively the Egyptian Pyramid of Principles:

East   Intelligence

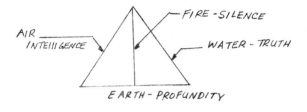

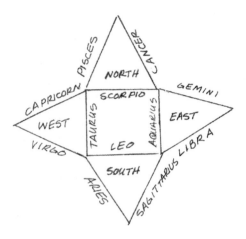

South	Silence
West	Profundity
North	Truth

In ancient times, before they were stripped of their casing stones, the sigils for these truths were actually carved into each of the sides.

These principles may sound familiar, for they have found their way into various Mystery Schools and metaphysical philosophies. Such as: the Masons, the Rosecrucians, Druidry, Wiccan, Coptic and even early Christian beliefs.

The pyramid was seen as a symbol of perfected humanity, the key to the meaning of life on this planet. What then, was the specific role of the Great and lesser pyramids in the Egyptian Mysteries?

Each pyramid represented a level of consciousness, which the initiate would have to master in order to become an enlightened being. Three levels, Physical-mundane, Emotional, Spiritual-Mental. The same three levels that were applied to the Egyptian Magical practices. These principles were reflected in the pyramids themselves starting with Mycerinus the smallest one, the pyramid of Khepper or the physical body. The Pyramid of Chephren the Ab or emotional body, and lastly, the pyramid of Khufu, the Sekhem or Spiritual body.

"It is the job of man to reach the eighth stage."
Tehuti

The Second Birth
To the neophyte, initiation is seen as a rite of passage in which he or she sheds a layer of earthly concerns. This in turn takes them one step further to perfection in their lifetime. The pyramid initiation, was the culmination of a process that took most initiates 30 years. Years of magical studies and service in the priesthood that lead up to this most holy of rites.

The pyramid initiation was not only reserved for the priesthood which consisted of both male and female, it was required of the Pharaoh himself. For the Pharaoh was required to be spiritually fit as well as physically fit in order to rule successfully as the living representative of God on earth.

To prepare for initiation, having completed the required magical studies, the initiate would fast on fruits and vegetables, abstaining from all flesh for one month. They would then shave and pluck all hair from their bodies including their eyelashes to symbolize their readiness to be reborn again from the womb. When this had been completed they would be ready to enter the pyramid complex.

The pyramid complex in ancient times would have been awesome sight to behold. A stone wall, of which only ruins remain today, would have surrounded it in its entirety. The complex itself, originally consisting of the pyramids and the Sphinx, was added to in the 4th and 5th dynasties to contain tombs and mastabas of that era. A long stone causeway led from the edge of the Nile river to the paws of the Sphinx. It was here that the initiate would undergo their first challenge before the fiery red visage of Her-Mem-Akhet, The Sphinx. It was a challenge in the form of questioning from the priests. If he or she passed the questioning, they would be allowed to enter through the door between the paws of the Sphinx to the secret art gallery below. The initiate would then proceed down a narrow stone passage to the smallest of the pyramids, Mycerinus the pyramid of Khepper, or the physical body. The initiate would be led to lie down in a black basalt sarcophagus and left for three nights. During those three nights he would undergo the trials of the physical body, hunger, cold, discomfort and pain all in total darkness. At the end of the third night he or she would be led once more underground, to the middle pyramid, Chephren the pyramid of the AB the emotional body. Here he would spend three nights as well, undergoing those trials of the emotional body such as fear, sentiment, anxiety and self-doubt.

If the initiate had passed successfully through the trials of the first two pyramids he or she would then be ready to undergo the trials of the Great pyramid, Khufu, the pyramid of the Sekhem or spiritual body. The Great pyramid contained not only one chamber but three; one underground below the surface and two located inside the pyramid itself. These three chambers duplicated once more the three levels of consciousness, physical, emotional, and spiritual.

The initiate would have to repeat them again, three nights in each, making his or her stay in the Great pyramid nine nights in all. After completing three nights in the Khepper chamber and three nights in the AB chamber the initiate would have sufficiently broken down the barriers that tied him to the conscious world, freeing the vessel that housed their soul. When at last the initiate lay down in the sarcophagus in the Sekhem chamber, Hemut, the Womb of the Second Birth, his or her soul would be free to journey to the stars. It would have two choices in its travels.

There are two airshafts in the Sekhem chamber, one points to the southern star (Sothis) Osiris and the cycle of reincarnation, and one pointed to the North Star and the Milky Way. If the soul or Khabit of the initiate traveled in the form of his or her astral body to the Sothis star, he or she would return back to earth to be reincarnated again. If their soul traveled north to the Milky Way, he or she would become perfected, god-like, and would never have to reincarnate again.

I imagine it was perhaps, not unusual for the priests to find on rare occasions, the earthly vessel of an initiate in the sarcophagus devoid of its life force.

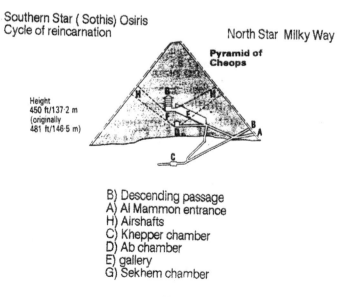

Southern Star (Sothis) Osiris
Cycle of reincarnation

North Star Milky Way

Pyramid of
Cheops

Height
450 ft/137·2 m
(originally
481 ft/146·5 m)

B) Descending passage
A) Al Mammon entrance
H) Airshafts
C) Khepper chamber
D) Ab chamber
E) gallery
G) Sekhem chamber

Pyramid Facts and Magical Attributes:

Height of the Great Pyramid: 450 ft (originally 481 ft with limestone casing) 365 steps to King's chamber, 365 ft from base to top on each side.

7 niches in the Grand Gallery, 7 stages in humankind's development,

7 spinal Chakras

Magical number: 5

5 Neters: Osiris, Isis, Set, Nepthys, Horus

Horus of the Horizon

What walks on four legs at dawn, two legs by day and three legs at sunset?

Riddle of the Sphinx

Let us not forget in our fascination with the Pyramids, the benevolent guardian that stands before them, a silent witness to mysteries beyond time and space, the Sphinx.

Her-Mem-Akhet, Horus of the Horizon whose face turned to the rising sun, embodies the foundation of the Egyptian Mysteries and the first step to initiation into the priesthood.

There have been many theories about the symbolism of the Sphinx. It has been speculated that with the body of a lion and the face of a man, the Sphinx represents the end of the age of Leo and rebirth in the Age of Aquarius.

What does this mean? Well it certainly could place the building of the Sphinx at the approximate time of the fall of Atlantis, 10,000 BC in the age of Leo, correlating it with the building of the pyramids as well. The head of the man, symbolizes the Age of Aquarius, which we are entering now, facing the east, the direction of the rebirth of the sun and a new day. Could this mean that the glory of the Age of Leo and Atlantis, will be reborn in the Age of Aquarius?

It has foretold, by the practitioners of the Egyptian Mysteries, that when the Sphinx dissolves into the sand, a great discovery of a hidden chamber will be found in its base. This chamber will be filled with ancient records that explain the building of the pyramids, astronomy, astrology and many other sacred sciences as well as beautiful works of art.

And it is clear that this day may be soon to come, for the Sphinx is deteriorating at an alarming rate year by year and all the modern technology has not been able to curtail it.

Authors and Egyptologists alike have sought to probe underneath the Sphinx to find the hidden chambers, only to be stopped short by Egyptian authorities. There have been small discoveries such as a statue found in one of the paws but nothing else so far. Could it be that society as a whole is not ready for that information to be revealed?

The practitioners of Egyptian Magic and the Isian Tradition believe this to be true.

Magical Attributes:

75 ft high, 120 ft long

Human head stands for intelligence

Neck of a Bull, indefatigable will

Body and paws of a Lion, courage and ability to fight to achieve a purpose

The Great Pyramid at Giza
March 13, 2000, Giza plateau and the Great Pyramid

It is our second day on Egyptian soil and we stand in wonder at the base of the greatest temple on earth, the Great Pyramid of Khufu/Cheops. Though I have been here many times before, the shear presence of the pyramid never fails to take my breath away.

Here inside the Sekhem/King's Chamber we will perform a very special ritual that will serve as a cosmic tuning fork, energizing us for the rest of our journey.

We have a short wait as our guide arranges for our entrance into the pyramid, time to notice the hustle and bustle around the pyramid complex. It is a popular spot for local school children to picnic during their lunch break, young lovers also find perches atop the giant stones to steal a flirtation. The tourist police with their white police camels pose for pictures with visitors, while a few sparse vendors pedal papyrus and other souvenirs.

When at last, it is our turn to enter the pyramid, we begin a brief ascent up the side of the pyramid to the only outside entrance, the Al Mammon entrance. Through here we will begin the strenuous climb up to the Queen and King's chambers. It is dark and silent, slightly stuffy and definitely not the place for the claustrophobic. It is however, proven to be the safest place on earth during an earthquake. The climb itself serves as an initiation, dominating our physical bodies, freeing our psyche to experience the intuitive messages that will be given to us this day...

Cone of Power Meditation

Imagine raising a cone of power inside the most powerful conductor of magical energy this world has ever seen?

Well, that is just the meditation that I have chosen to initiate our spiritual journey with, creating a pyramid within a pyramid using words of power to attune our bodies, minds and our Sekhem-life force with the ancient magic that still vibrates through Egypt.

What you will need:

Vanilla scented votive candles or Tea lights
Frankincense
1 opened bottle of red wine
Bread or Dates for libation

After traversing the last, narrow, stone passageway, we find ourselves finally in the Sekhem chamber, The Womb of the Second Birth, the place where those ancient initiates faced their most challenging trial. The chamber is bare except for the sarcophagus placed at one end. The ceiling of the chamber rises high above us, airshafts about a foot in diameter gape darkly at us from either ends of the chambers. The same airshafts, that point respectively, towards Sothis and the Milky Way.

After catching our breaths and a brief exploration of the chamber, we are ready for our meditation, for time is of an essence as we have only one hour of private time allotted to us.

An altar consisting of a pure white linen cloth, is set up in the very center of the chamber on the stone floor. This makeshift altar will have to do, as we are very limited with what we can carry into the pyramid.

The bottle of red wine is opened and placed on the altar along

with the libation, an incense burner filled with Frankincense is ignited in preparation so that its smoke will cleanse any negativity that may have been brought into the chamber by other travelers. The next things to be placed on our little altar are personal objects that we wish to empower such as Tarot cards, amulets, jewelry, crystals, scarabs and so forth.

When this is done I ask everyone to form a circle on the floor around the altar and place their candle in front of them. The candles are then lit one by one and the lights are turned off in the pyramid chamber.

We are cloaked in absolute darkness, the only illumination coming from our circle of candles. I ask everyone to join hands and then to take three cleansing breaths. The breathing is important for it nourishes the Sekhem force within us.

Still breathing evenly, we begin to visualize the Sekhem energy as a golden light coming from the middle of the earth up through our spine at the base or root chakra. We fill our bodies with the light then send it down our left arms to the person next to us. The golden light forms a circle from palm to palm. The energy moves around and around, from left to right in a sunwise or clockwise direction rising higher and higher until it forms a cone above our heads. It is then that I lead them in chanting the words of power.

I begin with "YOD" making sure to resonate the vowel so that it becomes a sacred vibration such as "YYYOOOODDD" the students repeat after me. Next is "HE" pronounced "HAY" then "VAU" pronounced "VOW" and then "HE" again. "YOD HE VAU HE", the ancient Hermetic invocation to summon the Gods of creation.

This chant is repeated five times, the sacred number of Tehuti the Divine Magi, going faster and faster, and building more and more energy. The words of power resonate through the chamber filling it and energizing us from head to toe. It is now time to take from that energy what our mind and body will need to heal it, transform it and energize it.

When this done, it is time to lower the cone of golden light, diminishing it until the golden light is once more centered in each one of us individually, it is then slowly released back down into the stones.

This is one of my favorite energizing meditations, and one I always perform in the Great Pyramid when I am in Egypt. I understand that it is not possible for everyone to perform this meditation in the Great Pyramid. However, it does not have to be done there exclusively. This meditation can be performed in your own sacred space or underneath a personal pyramid that you have constructed of your own.

Salute to Almighty Ra

This ritual is performed to give salute to the Sun God Ra, on his daily journey. Every day

Atum Ra sails his boat of a million years from the nighttime of the underworld up into the heavens in the form of the Sun Disc. Tehuti in his role as the 'Heart of Ra' accompanies him on this daily journey. In ancient Egypt the priests would perform this ritual four times a day, at dawn, noontime, dusk and midnight. When in Egypt, the students and I perform this ritual at high noon when the Sun crests over the top of the Great Pyramid. At home, I make it part of my daily rituals to salute the Sun during at least one of its four phases.

Ritual checklist:

A gold candle or Oil Lamp
Frankincense
An incense burner or Thurible
Acacia Oil or Olive Oil

If you are able to rise in the morning before dawn or as close to it as possible, begin by placing your candle or Oil lamp in the East, the direction of the rising Sun. Anoint your candle with the oil, if you are using the Oil Lamp put a few drops of the oil in with the lamp oil. Take three deep Sekhem breaths. Light your incense and meditate on what lies before you this day. When you are finished raise your arms in the KA position, above your head in salute. In clear resonate voice invoke the power of Ra.

> "Praise be to thee Almighty Ra, who cometh forth
> from the pillars of the Duat in the underworld to
> shine his golden splendor upon the Earth and the
> heavens above!
> Praise be to thee Almighty Ra!
> Praise be to thee his brother Tehuti!
> Hika! Hika! Hika! Hika! Hika!"

After you have spoken this invocation, take up your incense burner and begin to cense you sacred space starting in the East. Move sunwise or clockwise to the South, West, North and then back to the East.

Salute the East once more, then cross your arms in the Osiris position right arm over left across your chest and bow to the easterly direction once more. If you have chosen to do your ritual at noontime you will salute the Sun from the direction of noon, the south. If you have chosen dusk or midnight the ritual will be performed in the directions of the west and the north respectively. After bowing to the Sun in the Osiris position, recite these words:

"The Fire of Creation is born again,
Darkness is defeated and the light shall
Rule the heavens and earth below."

Scarab of the Vivified Heart

This magical scarab is created as an amulet to bring renewal of the Ab or heart to allow it to become open again to receive new love or to revive an old love. It can be worn over the heart, carried in your pocket or purse, or placed on your altar.

Your scarab amulet can be made of self-hardening clay, or carved in wood or stone and should be red in color. This amulet, as with all amulets, must be created during the waxing moon and empowered during the full moon. The top of the amulet should depict as close as possible the body of the Scarab beetle, the God of Creation Khepera. The bottom of the amulet should be inscribed with the hiero-glyphs for the Ab. In the center of the amulet are the sacred words for the vivifying of the heart.

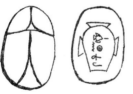

Ritual Checklist:

Rose Oil
Rose petals
Red Fimo clay
Natron water
Sandalwood incense
White or pink candle

On the night of the full moon begin by purifying your ritual space with Natron water from east sunwise to the north. Light the incense and the candle. Create your scarab out of the clay then put it into the oven to bake for the prescribed time. When it is done, remove it from the oven and let it cool completely. When your scarab is cooled anoint it with the first finger of your left hand, top to bottom with the rose oil. Light the candle, then 'show' your amulet to the flame so that it may animate it with life-force, as you do so, say these words:

"I am Tehuti the founder of medicines and letters,
Come to me, thou that art under the earth, Rise
Up to me! Thou Great Spirit!

When this is done take your scarab and hold it up to the east, and repeat these words:

"Hail ye who carry away hearts! Hail ye who steal hearts,
and make the heart of man go through its transformations
according to its deeds,
Let not what he hath done before harm him,
Homage to you O' ye Lords of Eternity,
Ye possessors of everlastingness, lead me O' Anpu forward so
that my heart be filled with love,
So it may spring forth anew like Bennu, the Soul of Ra!"

When you have completed the empowering of your scarab amulet you must wrap it in a small piece of red cloth, preferably silk or cotton until you are ready to use it. This ritual will bring renewal to your heart, and through that, love on all levels cannot help but be attracted to you.

Your Personal Pyramid

Your Personal Pyramid is a pyramid that you construct yourself. It is a powerful tool for use in meditation and magic. Through its mystical pyramidal shape, it will bring energizing and preserving qualities into your ritual space. Your cat will like to sleep under it as well!

It can be made from such simple materials as cardboard and construction paper or as elaborate as copper tubing mounted with a crystal. The paper pyramids can be made in colors according to purpose such as: Green for prosperity, red for action and passion, yellow for health and purple for psychic receptivity. The only major requirement is that you construct your pyramid to the proper scale such as in the following example.

Height	Base	Side
3"	4.71"	4.48"
4"	6.28"	5.98"
5"	7.85"	7.47"
6"	9.42"	8.98"
8"	12.57"	11.96"
10"	15.70"	14.95"
12"	18.85"	17.93"

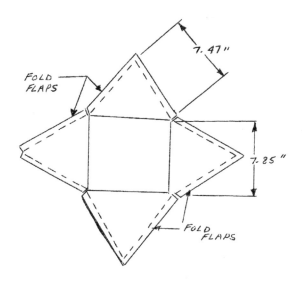

Pyramid Chakra Meditation

This meditation makes use of the pyramid as an energizing tool to activate the seven spinal Chakras. The Chakras are energy centers that lie along the spine at different intervals. Each Chakra has a color association and a physical, emotional and spiritual association as well.

Starting with the Base Chakra they are:

Chakra	Color	Rules	Astrological sign
Base Chakra	Red	Appendix, Kidney, Spinal cord	Sagittarius
Sacral Chakra	Orange	Reproductive organs	Capricorn
Solar Plexus	Yellow	Pancreas, Stomach, Liver, Gall Bladder, Nervous System	Scorpio
Heart	Green	Heart, Blood, Circulatory System	Libra
Throat	Blue	Thyroid, Lungs, Vocal Chords	Virgo
Brow	Indigo	Pituitary, Lower Brain, Left Eye, Ears, Nose, Nervous System	Leo
Crown	Violet	Pineal, Upper Brain, Right Eye	Cancer

The best size of pyramid to use in your meditation is between five to nine inches so that you can comfortably move it from Chakra to Chakra without strain, plain white cardboard is perfect.

To begin your meditation, lie quietly with your back on the floor or a firm surface. Take three deep cleansing breaths. As you do visualize breathing in a pure golden light, then exhale all the tensions and worries of the day in the form of a gray cloud.

Place your pyramid on your Base Chakra area. Visualize it as a glowing bright red disc, spinning in a clockwise motion. Breathe slowly and deeply. Move the pyramid up to the Sacral Chakra area repeating your motions. Energize each Chakra in turn; when you are finished, take a moment to absorb the energy you need. Then let the excess energy flow back down into the earth, grounding you.

This meditation can be done alone or with the assistance of a magical partner. It is a very powerful meditation and should not be repeated on a daily basis.

ANKUS UTA SENB

Journey's End

March 2000, Giza

As I stand before the paws of the Sphinx, a red-gold sunset bathes its benevolent face. The sun has set on our journey into the mysteries of Egyptian Magic. And yet, like the sun that sinks even now beneath the shadows of the great pyramids, it is not an end but a beginning. A beginning in which we will go forth renewed and energized from the power and presence of the Great Temples and the rituals that we have performed within their hallowed halls. The veils of mystery that we have lifted, and the blessings that we have received as we invoked the Gods and Goddesses. These things I feel are eternal and once awakened can never leave us, even if we are never to return to Egypt they will live inside our hearts forever.

Footnotes

Part 1
[3] The Gods and Symbols of Ancient Egypt, Manfred Lurker
[2] Chapter cxxiv, The Egyptian Book of the Dead

Part 2
[1] The Book of The Dead, E.A.Wallis Budge
[2] The Leyden Papyrus
[3] Chapter of the Buckle, E.A. Wallis Budge, Book of the Dead
[4] The Festival Songs of Isis and Nepthys, London 1898
[5] Chapter Ixxxii, The Egyptian Book of the Dead
[6] Chapter xxxvii, Egyptian Book of the Dead
[7] Chapter clxiv, the Egyptian Book of the Dead
[8] The Mysterious, Magical Cat, D.J. Conway
[9] The Gods and Symbols of Ancient Egypt, Manfred Lurker
[11] Chapter clx, the Egyptian Book of the Dead
[12] The Sirius Connection, Murry Hope
[13] Feasts of Light, Normandy Ellis

Bibliography

Aldred, Cyril, *Egypt to the end of the Old Kingdom*, London, Thames and Hudson, 1965.

Brier Bob, *Ancient Egyptian Magic*, New York, Quill, 1981.

Budge, E. A. Wallis, *The Book of the Dead*, New York: Dover 1967.

_____. *Egyptian Magic*, New York: Dover, 1971.

_____. *The Gods of the Egyptians, Vol I and II*, New York: Dover, 1969

_____. *The Egyptian Hieroglyphic Dictionary*, New York: Dover, 1978

Carpiceci, Carlo, *The Art and History of Egypt*, Florence Italy: Casa Editrice Bonechi, 2000

Conway, D.J., *The Mysterious Magical Cat*, St Paul: Llewellyn Publications, 1998

Dale-Green, Patricia, *Cult of the Cat*, New York: Weathervane Books

Ellis, Normandie, *Feasts of Light*, Illinois: Quest, 1999

Ellis, Normandie, *Awakening Osiris*, Grand Rapids, Phanes Press: 1988

Farrar, Janet and Stewart, *The Witches Goddess*, Custer: Phoenix Publishing, 1989

_____. *The Witches God*, Custer: Phoenix Publishing, 1989

Harris, Eleanor L., *Ancient Egyptian Divination and Magic*, York Beach: Weiser, 1998

Hope, Murry, *Practical Egyptian Magic*, New York: St. Martins Press, 1984

_____. *The Sirius Connection*, Great Britain: Elements Press, 1990

Lurker, Manfred, *The Gods and Symbols of Ancient Egypt*, London, Thames and Hudson, 1980

Murray, Margaret, *The Splendor that was Egypt*, New York: Preager

Printers, 1969

Sadhu, Mouni, *The Tarot*, North Hollywood: Wilshire Book Company, 1970

Schwaller, Lubicz, *The Egyptian Miracle*, New York: Inner Traditions International, 1985

Schueler, Betty and Gerald, *Egyptian Magick*, St. Paul: Llewellyn Publications, 1997

Silverman, David P., Lasko, Leonard H, Baines, John, *Religion in Ancient Egypt*, London: Cornell University Press, 1991

Thompson, Herbert, *The Leyden Papyrus*, New York: Dover, 1974

Tomkins, Peter, *Secrets of the Great Pyramid*, New York: Harpers and Row Publishers, 1971

Watterson, Barbara, *Women in Ancient Egypt*, Great Britain: Wren's Park Press, 1991

Wilkinson, Richard H., *The Complete Temples of Ancient Egypt*, New York: Thames and Hudson, 2000

West, Anthony, *The Serpent in the Sky*, New York: Julian Press, 1987

Witt, R.E., *Isis in the Ancient World*, Baltimore: John Hopkins Press, 1997